MAN DOWN

A JOURNEY WITH GOD, FAMILY, AND TOXIC MASCULINITY

DAVID JACKSON IV

Trilogy Christian Publishers
A Wholly Owned Subsidiary of Trinity Broadcasting Network
2442 Michelle Drive
Tustin, CA 92780

For information, address Trilogy Christian Publishing
Rights Department, 2442 Michelle Drive, Tustin, Ca 92780.
Trilogy Christian Publishing/ TBN and colophon are trademarks
of Trinity Broadcasting Network.
For information about special discounts for bulk purchases,
please contact Trilogy Christian Publishing.
Manufactured in the United States of America

10 9 8 7 6 5 4 3 2 1
Library of Congress Cataloging-in-Publication Data is available.
ISBN 978-1-63769-594-4
ISBN 978-1-63769-595-1 (ebook)

To my Butterscotch Jellybean,

Thank you for loving my broken pieces. Here's to living our lives like it's golden for a couple of forevers.

To my boys,

Only through your love have I finally become a man. I love you guys!

To my family,

Umm…sorry! Hope Thanksgiving isn't too awkward this year. Love ya!

ACKNOWLEDGMENTS

Whew, we just wrote a book y'all! I spent so long trying to find my purpose in life. Who knew it would be to just share my story? Well, my parents knew! To my parents, thank you immensely, from the bottom of my heart. It was your guidance and belief that allowed me to work my way through my toxic masculinity. Dad, I want to especially thank you for all that you have done to teach me what it really means to love your family and be a man. It is because of you I will spend the rest of my life trying to love my wife and kids as much as you did yours. If I can even become half the man you have been to me, I will be blessed. Thank you!

To my Butterscotch Jellybean, your love has seen me through many rough moments, and for this, I am forever grateful. I want to thank you for giving me the space to talk about our lives so openly. While our journey has been far from perfect, it is ours, and I'm honored to be able to do it with you. You will always be my greatest accomplishment. I love you, Kid!

To my brothers: Jawan Jr., Ronnie, Tare, Quinton, Hunter,

Jawan Sr., and Rell. How do I even begin to describe how my heart hurts that you guys are no longer in my life? While I understand what had to be done, I will never go a day without missing you. While I was... I promise you will never be too heavy.

To all of the men that I met along my way through the DOC system, thank you for being a part of the making of this book. To Uncle Bert, my mentor and my friend, thank you for all of your advice and wisdom. You have done so much for me; words will never be able to explain it. I can't wait to go to church with you when we get home!

Pastor Thomas, I doubt you will ever know the profound impact you had on me. It is because of you men began to seek God with all of their hearts. You, my friend, are what a man should be, thank you! Also, I'm still going to need you to hurry up and record that album—I need it!

To Reggie, London, Meek, Reese, Rich, P. Lowe, Mr. Wright, Lucci, Redy Rob, DC, PB, and Uncle Moe, thank you for all y'all love! I wrote this book with the help of each one of you. There was never a time that I didn't learn something about being a real man from y'all. I am blessed and honored to call y'all brothers. Here's to seeing each other on the other side! Love y'all!

TABLE OF CONTENTS

01 | MAN UP

How could this be art; it is entirely too flawed?

What do you do when you want to scream and people are watching? Can you cry and still be a man? How many times have you made yourself vulnerable just to be told to "man up?" I once heard that when you let babies cry it out, you are, in effect, not teaching them to self soothe but instead teaching them that no matter how much they cry, nobody cares and will never come to their rescue. I believe we have evolved this concept of thinking and have attached it to the male species. How often do we see young boys cry and say, "Stop crying like a little girl," or "Big boys don't cry," or my own personal favorite, "Man up." From inception, we teach those young men that their emotions are something to be avoided at all costs. So, it naturally becomes easier to bully than to cry, creating a string of violence that perpetuates throughout the male diaspora.

Now, understand, violence isn't just the act of physical force against someone but can, and most often will, represent itself as abusive use of power. While a young man may not resort to physicality to present his emotions, he may begin to convey his sentiment in the form of a series of different displays of masculinity. A term coined as "peacocking." A chest poked out, walking—peacocking. The overuse of curse words when in a heated situation—peacocking. And the one that has affected me most; the need to conquer and conquest the female species as trophies to be won—peacocking in its most primal and primitive form.

The saddest part about it all is that these are simple socially scripted productions of the cultural ideas about what it means to be a man, which is played for an audience of those well-versed in our contrived beliefs of what a man is and should be, not allowing room for these ideas to be optional, but causing them to become almost mandatory. And if one chooses to deviate, they then become susceptible to criticism from their peers; thus, furthering the importance of an effective peacocking talent. So, please allow me to take my feathers off, if only for a moment. I am a product of this very syndrome.

For years I suffered from a form of depression that was very well hidden from those around me but was ever-present in the way I maneuvered throughout my day. Simple disagreements turned into a battlefield of rejection and broken pride, which I manifested into varying levels of aggression. More often than not, I found myself fists clenched, ready, and willing to escalate to the next level. To this day, when I get extremely mad, I stand fist clenched with tears streaming down my face. For years I would always wonder, "Why am I crying? I'm not sad, nor am I scared. So why am I crying?" I believe that, subconsciously, I created a release valve. Just as one would release the pressure from a pipe, the same can be said about our emotions. Sometimes you must be willing and able to allow for your vulnerability to escape.

I can remember one Thanksgiving when I was a teenager. We woke to water pooled in the basement of my parents' home. Oh, and when I say "pooled," I mean this water was probably ankle deep. After looking all over the house, trying to figure out who was going to get a whoopin' for leaving the water running, we figured out that it was one of the pipes in the wall that burst due to it being connected to the outside spigot and freezing over.

Take a moment to think about that; as night fell, the sun or the heating source was eliminated, leaving the cold air to intensify. The air then attacked the only vulnerable spot in the house's well-built defenses, freezing the access water lying dormant in the pipes. Once the water froze, it became too much for the pipe to handle, causing a buildup of pressure and then, ultimately, failure, resulting in thousands of dollars of damage and a very somber Thanksgiving weekend.

When we subscribe to the toxicity of the alpha male mentality, we are, in essence, cutting ourselves off from our main heating source—successful and open relationships with others—causing the cold air of our own insecurities to intensify and mount an attack on our most vulnerable of spots, freezing the inner workings of our emotions. Thus, beginning the process of building up pressure in our lives and ultimately leading to failure.

In response to the pipes freezing, my mother grabbed some old washcloths and a few rubber bands. She instructed me to cover each water spigot, in effect sealing the vulnerabilities from the harsh air of the outside world. You see, we, just as those pipes, don't need much. We don't need some expensive magical fix. Basically, all we really need is someone to help cover our most vulnerable places. The issue is most men, just as those pipes, often lack the ability to be able to tell someone they are in distress, often leading to help only coming once a catastrophic failure has been reached.

We must become acutely aware of the effects of the "man-up" culture we have allowed ourselves to succumb to. We, as men, have associated emotions with weakness so much that even in the writing of this book, I found myself anxious that you—the reader—would challenge my masculinity completely because of the way my vulnerability speaks so loudly through the chapters. You may possibly see me as a culmination of all the mistakes you will come to learn along your journey through this work. I asked myself, "What should I tell you? How much? And what is okay to leave out?" The answer is nothing. It is dire that we get to a point where we allow our faults to become our defining features. Walk proudly in the things that made you who God has called you to be.

In my early twenties, while dating this artsy young

lady, I recall being introduced to the art walk in the Dupont Circle area of Washington, DC. As a quasi-gang member, trouncing around an art show with a glass of wine and some brioche hors d'oeuvres didn't really feel quite right. Yet, in the midst of my feeling like I didn't belong, I happened to come across a canvas that seemed to cut through the muck and mire that was the noise of my underline insecurities.

Now, let me set this scene for you. There I stood, awkwardly holding a cup full of wine that I refused to drink (because thugs don't drink wine!), a plate laced with hors d'oeuvres that I couldn't quite figure out what it was even made of, and nodding in full agreement to whatever the young lady I happened to be trying to bed at that moment was saying. All the while stuck looking at this picture. Which, at first glance, was far from what I assumed the average art fan would deem a masterpiece. And yet, speaking to me amongst all of these beautifully painted landscapes, flowers, animals, and churches, there hung a canvas that would come to define the story of my existence. Unlike those landscapes, this painting seemed chaotic, almost even rushed. The brush strokes unorthodox, the colors having no central theme. How could this be art? It is entirely too flawed.

Standing in the middle of the piece was what I could only assume to be a man playing the saxophone. The word "Stardust" etched in an arch over his head. What one had to do with the other, I have yet to figure out, but it was breathtaking. As I became more entranced with the work, I can remember pulling out my phone to search its origin. "Stardust," read the title on the placard by some lady named Jean Michele Basquiat. After a quick web search, I quickly discovered I was wrong in my archaic assumption. This was actually the name and work of a young man who surprisingly looked much like me—black. The young lady I had almost forgotten I was with then said to me, "Oh, I love this artist." Sensing the preoccupied and disconnected tone in my "uh-huh," she left me there to decipher why I was so mesmerized.

On the ride home to go fulfill yet another one of my misdirected falsely identified "manly conquests," the aforementioned young lady said something that probably became the basis on which this book was built. "David, the reason I enjoy Basquiat's work is the very same reason I enjoy you: the beauty is in the abstract. When you view the painting in pieces, you may get lost in the chaos. But when taken in its entirety, you begin to find the wonder in its imperfections." Can you see the wonder in your imperfections, or are you too worried about having to "man up"?

Insecurities have riddled the majority of my days on this earth, and through the lens of man, I continue to see just how much I may not compare to the next guy. Then I am reminded that I am God's Stardust. I am His abstract work of unorthodox brush strokes, mismatched colors, and I'm sure others, just as I did, are wondering, "How could this be art? It is entirely too flawed." Psalm 139 says that God formed our inward parts and goes on to say that we are fearfully and wonderfully made. When we come to fully embrace God as the ultimate designer of our flaws, they become less of flaws and more of unique attributes that God clearly has need of.

This is a good enough time as any to explain to you that in no way, shape nor form am I smart enough to tell you how to live your life. But I have "man'd up" enough to tell you how not to. Along this journey of God, family, and toxic masculinity, you will be challenged, just as I was, to look at your vulnerabilities, not as insecurities, but as badges of honor. Let's get started!

02 | UNSTABLE

Have you changed? Or did they just catch you as your wardrobe malfunctioned?

Around the age of twelve, I began to run away from home. Not as an escape from some horrific childhood or some latent abuse that hung over my existence, but merely because I believed the world to be abundant with some form of love I couldn't seem to garner in my current space. You see, at the tender age of twelve, I found myself needing to feel something I couldn't yet say out loud. Now, understand I wasn't your stereotypical preteen. At twelve, I stood six-foot-one inch tall and a solidly built two hundred thirty pounds. So, while I had the mind of a child, my stature told me that I was a full-grown man. Which is more, sociological norms told me that you ain't a man until you have a woman. So, while my parents offered me unconditional love, they couldn't offer the love that would cement my place amongst the "real men."

Armed with the body of a man and the mind of a child, I began to scour near and far for the solidification of my manhood. Unbeknownst to my parents, I began to sit on a local free phone chat line for hours under the moniker Jazzlee. That then only fueled my need for acceptance from the female species, thus leading me to different online chatrooms.

After beginning to build up a cache of what I deemed to be suitable companions, I began to become emboldened in my charade. My need for acceptance became a constant whaling siren in the depths of my subconscious, urging me to feed the desire with the same exuberance that a vampire would lust for blood. And just as vampires aren't real, neither was acceptance. It seemed the harder I looked, the more it became an allusive figment of my imagination. For every young lady, I hoped would make me a man, I became more lost in the toxicity of what I believed manhood to be.

I spent so much effort in the conquest of manhood that I never took the time to create a working definition for myself. Define manhood, go ahead, I'll wait. I'm sure you, like I, struggle to define it without a bunch of arbitrary smashed-together one-liners like, "Manhood is the act of being a man," or "Manhood is when you do what you have to as a man."

Reality is, manhood must be defined not by your cultural upbringing but by your moral compass. The question becomes, "What happens when your moral compass tells you a man is two different things?" Thus, the conundrum I found myself in at the ripe age of twelve. The world around me told me that a man was defined in the difficulty of his conquest, his proficiency in spaces of elevated conflict or combat, and his ability to please the opposite sex, while my parents defined manhood through the lens of Christian concepts. A man is to leave his mother and father and find a wife. A man is to love his wife as Christ loves the church. And that a man is to provide and protect his family through noble means. Here I found myself confused. How can I find a wife and have multiple conquests? How does one become proficient in the pleasing of the opposite sex when he can't have sex until married?

Subsequently, I began to walk in both directions simultaneously. As you would assume, this left me lost and wandering aimlessly without purpose. You see, with the ease of a migrating bird, I would pick up from one situation and land in another without ever taking the time needed to consult my moral compass. Hence causing a rift in my emotional fabric because I couldn't just define manhood, but I couldn't define David. So, since I didn't know who I was or who I was meant to be, I became everything for everybody. Duality became nothing more than a costume change; it was nothing to be a hardcore gang member on Saturday and the son of a preacher on Sunday.

As I stated before, there was a time when I was a chronic runaway. There had never been a time when my parents weren't worried that when they came home, I wouldn't be there. But let's stop calling it "running away" because there was nothing I was running away from, but it was more about what my misguided mind thought I was running to. I can remember a time in one of my many exoduses from my parents' safety, where I had come to be introduced to a young lady through one of my past journeys. This young lady had to have been at least ten years my senior, but as I said, I was built like a man. In being introduced to the young lady, she asked me what my name was, and thugs aren't named David, so I told her, "Keyjaun." While I knew that the name David meant "Beloved of God" and that King David was inherently a warrior, I assumed, to be respected, I must have a more unique name.

What is interesting about this story is, right around this time, my father had spent multiple conversations with me imparting the importance of one's name. This topic became such a thing for my father that he even crafted a sermon titled "There is something in a name." Yet, when given the opportunity to be proud of my calling, I migrated to my other form and began to peacock.

W. E. B. Du Bois once spoke of double consciousness, a "sense of always looking at one's self through the eyes of others, of measuring one's soul by the tape of a world that looks on in amused contempt and pity." He went on to describe this phenomenon as a "two-ness"—a duality of sorts. A man having two masters, two minds, two moral compasses. So, while I knew I was David and beloved of God, I just had to make sure she knew I was Keyjaun and beloved of man.

The Bible says that a double-minded man is unstable in all his ways. That would probably explain why I couldn't seem to ever find the acceptance on which my search was predicated. While my journey always led to the doors of physically open women in which who never really allowed for emotional availability, because I was told that big boys don't cry, and she was told to find a man just like her daddy who probably, just like me, couldn't define manhood either. This unstable nature isn't something that I suffered from alone; it is something that reverberates throughout the male diaspora just as commonly as facial hair.

Instability ravaged the dark spaces of my youth, a swiftly metastasizing cancer, changing the structure of my emotions in its wake. I was not only a double-minded man, worse I was a double-minded boy. As shown previously, just giving my name was a tumultuous battle of warring ideals. The sad part is that that wasn't the depth at which my confusion displayed itself.

As stated, I am the son of a preacher, and believe me when I say my mother is a praying woman. However, it seemed that the more my faith in God grew, the louder the streets began to call. You see, I was the kid who used to gather all his toys around like an auditorium and preach until at least one of the Power Rangers got saved. Yet, I couldn't seem to remember those very words when it was my soul up for grabs. No matter the depth in which I fashioned my sermonic encouragements, I could never quite find the sequence of words that would activate stability in my life.

While in the seventh grade, I began to become acutely aware of my differing circumstance than that of my fellow male peers. While most of the young boys I befriended were navigating through life without the steady hand of a father, mine was an ever-present fixture in mine. While they lacked supervision due to an overworked, often single, mother, my mother was the poster child for being all in your business.

I can remember having a friend who I used to have such an affinity for because, like I, he was bigger in stature and looked well beyond his thirteen years of age. We used to rip and run the streets, getting into whatever mischief we could summon. While he was almost the mirror image of me physically, in terms of family, we couldn't have been any more different. Being reared up by his grandmother, he, unlike me, didn't have any of his biological parents around. His grandmother, being up there in age, did the absolute best she could in preparing him for the harsh reality of life, but that very same age worked against her causing her to become exhausted earlier in the day, leaving my friend and me to our own thirteen-year-old devices. We would eat what we wanted, come in the house whenever we wanted, and better yet, got to curse and speak however we wanted. This right here, this was manhood.

It was while hanging out with this friend that we began to wonder more about our culture. Yet, in Washington State, there isn't much by way of African American culture. So, we searched for the first group of men that looked like us. Sadly, the representation we found happened to be the gang that laid claim to the streets on which we grew up. It was then that my duality began to encourage me to take it up just a notch. Soon after, my friend and I were jumped onto a local neighborhood Crip set determined to be the baddest gangstas to ever do it.

Let's pause there. Two young boys interested in their culture become gang members, persistent on being the biggest and baddest, tough guys the streets had ever seen. Stop me when you begin to see where this is going. Duality is dangerous. Not before too long will it begin to breed dissension within one's conscious. We begin to blur the line between right and wrong, causing the very same kid who preached to Power Rangers to walk around with guns at thirteen. Maybe you, like I, know what it feels like to trade your calling for a costume, forcing yourself to become the very same person you were placed on this earth to help.

So, back to scheduled programming. As fully initiated members, we began to focus on maximizing the level of acceptance we could amass. My friend and I were destined to become men. We were finally becoming proficient at hand-to-hand combat, we had girls, and I was quickly learning how to please them. Yet, why did I still not feel like a man? My assumption was that if surveyed by anyone well-versed in the topic, they would quickly surmise that I was pretending. Because, no matter how much debauchery I got into Monday through Saturday, Sunday allowed me to go back to being that kid who preached to Power Rangers.

Every Sunday, I would rise to the melodic rhythms of gospel music vibrating throughout the house, serving as a reminder that today was going to be a good day. Today, I didn't have to worry about carrying the weight of my unforgiving costume. Today, I could be a thirteen-year-old kid who just wanted to hang out with his family. Today, I didn't worry about Keyjuan or his manhood. Today, I was free to allow God to see my emotions.

The reality is that we as men often find ourselves emotionally oppressed by our own ideals and precepts. Thus, leaving us feeling powerless, causing susceptibility to violent outbursts. Once again, I repeat, violence must not always be physical; it often is not. We must begin to recognize our duality and name it as such in efforts to mitigate its effect on our lives. While mine manifested in my persona, yours may live in your relationship or your career. How many times has someone told you that you have changed or that you're different somehow? Have you changed? Or did they just catch you as your wardrobe malfunctioned?

It is of dire importance that we, as men, begin to embrace emotion and bask in the release that it allows us. I once heard of a disease that doesn't allow for the afflicted to feel pain; in my ignorance, I wondered why would that be a disease? Come to find out that pain is the body's way to alert you to there is a problem. If you were unable to read those warnings, you would continue to walk on a broken leg which, in essence, would cause more damage. Yet, we attempt to turn off our emotional intelligence receptors, thus causing us to try and love on a broken heart. The damage, often cases, becomes unrepairable, breeding disdain, general social rejection, and loneliness.

It is not too late for your healing to begin. Now that we have identified the unstable nature of operating within a space of duality, we must begin to wholeheartedly participate in the creation of emotional availability within our lives. A double-minded man is unstable in all his ways. I choose stability, how about you?

03 | ABUSE IS INEVITABLE

I could hear the harmony of my purpose. Its silhouette never became clear.

Sometime after my friend and I released our innocence to the gang, I began to leave home with much more frequency and zeal. One night, after being tracked down at this friend's house by my father, my mother asked me, "Why would you leave your own bed and room to go sleep in somebody's closet?" I most definitely couldn't look my mother in her face and tell her that it wasn't the closet that I so richly desired; it was the intoxication of manhood. She just wouldn't understand. So, I gave her my customary "I don't know" in hopes that it would buy me a reprieve from the ensuing talking that I was sure was about to commence. Just as scripted, my mother began to outline to me all of the things that I was blessed to have in this life I was given, but why could she not understand that I would have traded it all for just one opportunity to call myself a man, and mean it?

After hours of listening to my mother with uninterested ears, I recall laying down for the night, wondering when it would finally be my moment. After what I could only assume to be on and off fits of laborious slumber, I awoke to yet another day of undefined purpose. Who was I meant to be today? Surely there was more for me than the bowels of my middle school hallway. So, it was at that moment that I decided that the only way to actualize my deeply rooted desire was to circumvent God and forge my own purpose.

Out of my youthful ignorance, I believed that purpose was something that could be manipulated at my hand. That my talents were nothing more than byproducts of my forced desires; if I want it bad enough, it will happen because I dictate my future. What I forgot to tell myself was that, in order to forge purpose, you must first breathe life into the fire, a skill that God has yet to teach me.

Dr. Myles Munroe once said that "when purpose is unknown, abuse is inevitable." The tragedy befalls this story when light is brought to the fact that purpose was undefined in my life until I began to pen this book. Purpose danced unobtainable through my life with the grace of a classically trained ballerina swaying through the shadows of my psyche to the symphony of my nerve-laden heartbeat. For every graceful leap of the ballerina's feet accompanied a thud to the drum of my emotions. Because, although I could hear the harmony of my purpose, its silhouette never became clear. Abuse is inevitable.

When asked how a young boy from a good family becomes a gang member, the answer is simple—undefined purpose. I operated in a space of being unaware of who I was called to be.

So, regardless of what others believed for me, I couldn't see beyond my lust for manhood to the well of purpose that laid dormant within me.

Although, sadly for my friend and me, it wasn't long before the inevitability of abuse came to roost at our feet. After about a year post-entrance into organized crime, while at a local neighborhood park, we were summoned to a car by one of the set's original founders. Enthused at the premise that this man knew who we were, my friend and I made haste to the waiting door of what would come to be our chariot of subjugation. With every footstep, we unknowingly embraced oppression with the glee of a minor child on Christmas morning. With every nervous look stolen between my friend and me, we began to sign over the deed to our emotional well-being. What is more to us, we were finally going to become men. Mere minutes later, while tucked into the throne of what I believed to be my manhood, I was instructed by the driver to grab something from under the seat. Upon reaching into the darkened space, my hand found nothing but cold metal from which I believed to be the undercarriage of the front passenger's seat.

After further inspection, I began to pull at the metal, bringing to birth a twin set of pistols with every identifying maker shaved off of them. With nervous wonder, I began to hand them to the operator of the vehicle and was met with a simple "nah, those are for y'all." After a brief moment of contemplation, I handed the weapon to my friend and began to ask the driver what we needed guns for. As the driver wound through the streets of the city, he took a brief pause and told me, "Man up, we got business to handle."

Too scared to question the operator of the vehicle, my friend just looked at me with a smile that I had never see from him; he, unlike I, was excited for what was sure to follow. As the surrounding scenery began to become more and more unfamiliar, I could only assume we had entered into rival territory. The boys standing on the corner who would customarily wear blue were now starting to wear red, yet, beyond their clothing, I noticed one thing, that they looked just like me—young black boys fixated on the proving of their manhood. As the car inched closer to its desired destination, I was told to get out and stand and watch at the corner.

Upon my exit from the vehicle, I noticed a car that looked oddly familiar, pulling alongside the car in which I had just gotten out of. As if somewhere someone yelled "action," the scene began to come alive with the sounds of a blockbuster action picture. Clashes of thunder accompanied bullets ripping through sheet metal as if pieces of paper. Screams played out a soundtrack of destruction and chaos, and there I stood, unable to help. The word "cut" would have done nothing for this situation because by the time I could find words, the familiar car pulled off into the setting sun with a trail of inevitability behind it.

Unable to move, I heard a good Samaritan yell for someone to call the police, that the people in the car had been hit. An inability to comprehend the situation began to fall on me, causing panic to set in. There I stood with a blue shirt and gun on the corner of an unknown street in blood territory. I quickly tucked in my shirt and zipped up my jacket, and walked briskly in the direction in which we had come.

Hoping that nobody noticed me in the commotion, I walked head down, scared to look back, all the while telling myself, *"Man up, big boys don't cry."* After what felt like a century, I finally stopped to evaluate my current situation. Scared and alone, I could only think of one thing, *Where was God when I needed Him?* Not remembering my circumvention of God's design, I began to ask God why He would do this. As I pen this missive to you now, I am stunned in the realization that, as long as things went right, I was the grand author of that fable, but at the moment things went bad, God was to blame for my misgivings.

Standing on that corner in what could possibly be titled clinically as "shock," I began to scream violently, swinging sporadically through the air, with full intention of showing God who was boss. After the realization that people may be looking, I proceeded to devise my plan. I couldn't go home because my mother, like always, would know exactly what question to ask to disengage my stoic disposition. So, I reverted to what I knew best, perpetrate manhood. Within minutes, I was standing at a gas station on the payphone dialing the number to the phone chatline in which I'd come to cherish. After a couple of hours of useless chatter, I happened across the voice of a woman who would come to be the matron of my demise.

Melodic and sultry came the voice through the receiver, exciting my still frazzled senses. After some time of shared interests and laughter, she asked me what I was going to do with the rest of my night. Undecided if going home was yet an option, I devised a story in hopes of garnering a level of sympathy. I explained that due to a nasty argument between my family members and myself, I was currently homeless, so I would be on this payphone until the next day in which I would be traveling to another state to go live with distant relatives. Upon the receipt of my mistruth, she quickly asked where I was, stating that she had her own abode and would be more than open to allowing me to stay with her for some time. Excited by the prospect, we started to work through how to reach her home via the metro bus system, and a mere hour later, I was knocking at her door.

Now, remember, I had only spoken to this young lady over a phone, so as my hand made contact with the faded green chipping paint of the apartment door, I was clueless to what existed just on the other side. Soon after my cadence of equally spaced knocks, I was rewarded by the sound of the locking mechanism disengaging. As the door crept open in a dramatic fashion, I was surprised at what I saw standing in the amber glow of the doorway. She was stunning.

Even at thirteen, I had a healthy understanding of beauty and often considered myself a connoisseur of sorts. In astonishment, I stood there awkwardly, awaiting this mirage to dissipate. After a brief once over, my femme fatale nodded her head in approval, made a comment to my boyish charm, and escorted me into her lair.

Unsure of my physical aptitude in her opinion, I began to ratchet my peacock up to mass effect, allowing for my plumage of deception to cover any weakness that may lie bare before her. Nervous and anxious, I made sure to stand tall, with my chest poked out, flexing every muscle in my body that I could engage. Only to be met with a "Relax. You're safe now." Unsure of why my companion believed me to feel unsafe, I did as she requested and relaxed. As if removing the plug from a drain, the moment I relaxed, my emotions came flowing out of me. Tears ran down my face between hyperventilated breaths. With fist-clenched hands, I began to aggressively wipe at the streams of agony that glistened down my cheeks. As if asked by the universe my plight, I told everybody, or nobody, "They killed my brother, cuz."

Without the recoil of shock I expected, she grabbed my hand with a seductively measured amount of pressure and, as if a spectator in the galley of my life, simply said, "Man up. I'm gonna make you feel better." Abuse is inevitable.

04 | LIPS DRIP HONEY

The hands of the abused man fashion oppression.

I awoke to the smell of lavender laced with a sweetness I couldn't quite place. After gathering my thoughts, I quickly looked for the pants that concealed the gun given to me just the day before. After confirming that the weapon was still hidden in my pocket, I went to search for the woman I had come to desire. As I got closer to the kitchen, the sweet smell began to permeate my senses; what could that possibly be?

Bending the corner into the kitchen, I was surprised to see my host standing over a stove, staring intently at whatever she was cooking. As if on cue, the piercing whine of a tea kettle began to cut the silence of the morning's peace. Just then, she looked at me with a devilish grin and motioned for me to come to her. As I nervously approached, she asked if I wanted some tea with my breakfast. Not being very fond of tea, I declined and inquired if that was the smell that had woken me from my slumber. "Lavender honey tea. I drink it every morning," she whispered in a voice that I could only describe as tantalizing. If only then I knew that I would come to hate the smell of honey.

After enjoying the final bites of my breakfast, I looked up to her gaze. Quickly assuming I had let my guard down, I sat up and said, with the deepest voice I could muster, "What?" With almost a chuckle, she said, "So, how old are you really?" Nearly choking on my food, the only answer I could think of on the spot was the truth. "Thirteen," I said with hopes of a soft landing. After a moment of silence and held breaths, she looked at me and said, "Good. I'll have fun making you a man."

Allow me to add some color to this narrative, if I may. There I stood, thirteen years old, marred by the trauma that held the final breath of my closet friend, in the presence of a woman that I had just met hours before in a fit of post-traumatic stress. My conscious ate away at the tattered strings of my morality, becoming an ever-present reminder of who I was and who I had become. At thirty-six, by far, she was the oldest woman I had ever been involved with, which is more, she believed in my ability to be a man.

You see, by the age of thirteen, I was so enamored with the societal concept of being a man I willingly traded my innocence for bullets, my curiosity for ignorance, and my soul for sex. The Bible says in Proverbs that the "lips of an adulterous woman drip honey," and I quickly was stuck in the tar textured substance.

After only a few hours of lighthearted banter, things began to turn. As a song began to play on the radio that reminded me of my friend, reality came roaring back, riding the swells of a tsunami of emotions. All at once, my temperature began to rise, causing an instant state of agitation and discomfort. Before my host could sense my aggregating emotions, I told her that I needed to leave, and I appreciated her hospitality. With the same spontaneity that my emotions surged, she became cold and dark, almost sinister. "You can't go anywhere until I'm done with you." Her words landed with the precision of an archer at point-blank range.

Unsure if I misjudged the tone of her jest, I laughed and began to walk towards the door. As if born with the agility of a leopard, she jumped in my way and repeated her comment, making sure I fully understood that this was no laughing matter. As questions of "what now?" began to ricochet through my brain, I thought about the gun in my pocket. *Should I? No, but maybe just to scare her.* As if reading my mind, she proceeded to explain to me that she was aware I had a gun, and if I didn't want her to call the police, I must do exactly what she said. Fear began to paralyze my body. While I wasn't new to criminal activity, jail seemed like something that I couldn't quite handle.

Unwillingly, I began to mentally relinquish control over my choices. For the next two days, I became a robot of sorts, a toy devoid of emotion programmed to meet the demands of a deviant operator. I was made to perform acts from sexual to household chores, all while being told I was going to make such a good man for her. As evening fell on the third night, there was something in the air that seemed different.

There was a peace that often seems to come before the storm. As if summoned by my thought, my captor instructed me to lie down on the bed. After restraints were bound around my limbs, I fought back the tears and the urge to cry. *Man up, big boys don't cry.*

Within minutes of my being affixed to the bed, I began to feel pressure below my waist. Unable to breathe between sobs of restrained tears, I began to feel the worse pain I had ever felt. After what felt like a lifetime, I was finally left alone, tears streaming down my face; all I could do was silently cry. *Man up, big boys don't cry.* Upon collecting my breath, I began to feel a warmth pooled under my body. Scared that fear had caused me to urinate myself, I quickly surmised that it was something much more sinister; it was blood.

While laying there in a pool of blood, I began to savagely shake at the restraints. I pulled at each of them with all of my might. After a few unsuccessful tugs, I began to frantically scream for help. With every scream, I became more and more aware of the fact that nobody even knew I was there. The screams for help fell on deaf ears, thus leaving my only chance at survival to be my own strength. With more violent pulls at the supports, I was able to break the bonds in which held me captive. Once again, I found myself head down, swiftly moving away from a scene in which took the innocence from a young boy.

Does honey have you captive? Or have you broken the bonds? Truth is, too often, we as males fail to speak about our trauma; in the reading of these words will be the first time my parents or my wife will learn this story. While they didn't know the story, they knew the trauma. Due to honey, I spent most of my days fixated on never being disrespected nor taken advantage of again. I promised myself at the moment that I would always fight for my manhood. If ever given the chance again, I would have not only pulled my weapon; I would have used it.

My trauma told me that I would never be a man. A man would never allow himself to be abused. If I was stronger, maybe, just maybe, I could have stopped her. Maybe I could have stopped the bullets that ended my friend's life. Maybe, if I was stronger, I would be a man.

Sadly, I have come to learn that a lot of young males are the victim of emotionally debilitating abuse, yet many never say a word. More often than not, we suppress the emotions only to be acted out in fits of misguided anger and oppressive actions of our own. The popular term "hurt people hurt people" comes to mind in demonstrating this phenomenon.

Due to my experiences, I became cold in the facilitation of emotions. Love and warmth became topics as foreign to me as quantum physics. My moral compass, which always pointed true north, began to fluctuate in its readings, causing misdirected movements to become the norm. It was on that day that I began to journey through life with the assistance of an uncalibrated GPS. White became black, and black became white, while right became varying levels of wrong, and wrong became survival. *Man up, big boys don't cry.*

Although the lips of the adulterous woman drip honey, the hands of the abused man fashion oppression. We must open ourselves to the vulnerability needed to seek assistance in our healing. With the same veracity that we regard our manhood, we should begin to explore the depths of our emotional well-being. Mental health not just being some crackpot design trumped up by money-hungry doctors, but a vital part of one's ability to meet a holistic closure.

Victory is yours, says the Lord, but never were you told you didn't have to fight for it. To reach a place of healing, you must be willing to take inward inventory of your darkest spaces. Now I understand better than most that some of these spaces are places that you may not have seen in a long time. The moans of tattered hearts echo deep in the vast expanses of your broken pieces. You get excited as hopes and dreams flash across the skies like shooting stars only to find that, just as stars, they are so close, yet so far away. You can hear the voice of your mother say that joy comes in the morning, but all you want in this dark space is a night light.

While this place is often ugly and reminiscent of harder times, we must learn how to navigate within its confines. You see because darkness and light can never exist in the same spaces. We must be adamant in speaking light to the darkness, allowing for the very same thing that disqualified you to now become your qualification. While the lips of the adulterous woman drip honey, the blood of a loving savior flows healing.

05 | A FATHER'S LOVE

He wasn't the man I had thought he was, and he was the man God knew he was.

After a year, I became proficient in the art of hiding my trauma, or so I believed. Oftentimes, the trauma was hidden only to me. My festering wounds became emblazoned beacons of unmitigated hurt. The people around me noticed the underlying symptoms yet couldn't seem to figure out the antidote to what ailed me. Due to my fixation with proving my male prowess, I began a calculated assault on what I deemed to be the soft places of my heart. I systematically began to remove anything that questioned my dominance, picking off the remnants of adolescence in my wake.

Love became a word I loathed, not even willing to share it with the family I valued so. Anger, the emotion I wore like a cape, meant to shield my vulnerabilities from the risk of compromise. I began to construct my foundation on the quicksand of depression. Sinking further as each day passed, unable to voice my need for assistance. *Man up, big boys don't cry.*

As you would assume, my academic enrichment was downgraded in juxtaposition to the furtherance of my social standing. The hallowed title "Big Man on Campus" became not only my least common denominator but my absolute zero. While I excelled in many things in school, such as language, arts, and sports, it often always took a backseat to my social agenda.

Quickly I'd arrived at a position where school began to get in the way of my bolstering manhood. Causing my premature exit, while not officially dropping out, my presence often came as a surprise. This truancy began to get so bad my parents modified their schedule in order to make sure I made it to school on time. With the same assurance my parents had that they personally saw me walk into the school, I had the knowledge that the backdoor was always open.

I wonder today how many men operate through their lives always aware of the backdoor's availability. Never quite content with where they are but always aware of the exits. Maybe you're better than I, and you haven't succumbed to the fallacy of the grass always being greener. Or maybe you were too wise to quit your job knowing you didn't have another lined up, but that's okay because you're not going to let anybody talk to you like that. Or maybe, just maybe, you're more like me than you care to admit, and you, too, have identified your exit in case of emergency.

They say in America that half of all marriages end within the first three years. I wonder how many of those people only got married because they knew that divorce was an option. If I may submit for your consideration that we as men must begin to live our lives understanding that there are no exits, only stairways, and we have the choice in which direction to climb.

Throughout my sophomore year of high school, I began to escalate in terms of my mischievous deeds, climbing deeper down the stairs of despair. Soon enough, I was stealing cars—the victims most often being my family. After numerous felony traffic stops that lead to a few weeks in juvenile, my parents began to grow tired of my antics. If only they could have understood that men had cars and I needed to be a man.

Operating under that misnomer, I once again, in the dead of night, started my father's car with plans of grandeur. I had already planned my route the night before with my latest mixtape burnt CD in hand—manhood, here I come.

After a day of driving around town with the windows down and the music loud, I began to notice the emptiness in which this often-busy thoroughfare possessed. Putting the thought out of my mind, within minutes, I was surrounded by multiple unmarked police cars with guns drawn, instructing my swift removal from the vehicle. Sadly, this was just another insistence for me. Within days, I would be released, fully aware that, although I was walking in the front door, the back was always open.

This time though, something was different. After a couple of weeks, I was taken to court to stand trial for what I had done. Unsure of what was going to happen, I was able to breathe easier when my father walked in. Just as he had done for many years previous, here he was, to rescue me from myself. Only, this time, it wasn't how I expected. After the judge asked my father if he had any words before my sentence was levied against me, he stood up, sauntered to the podium, and proceeded to eradicate my belief in his support of me. My father, the quintessential alpha male, with sorrow in his voice and the makings of tears in his eyes, told the judge that I wasn't learning from my previous follies and needed to be given real jail time in efforts to get the help that I needed.

With the thud of the judge's gavel, I became a ward of the Juvenile Rehabilitation Administration for the following fifty-two to sixty-four weeks. Within weeks of that day, I was whisked onto a handcuffed transport ride to a juvenile facility labeled an institution. Through the twang of country music, rushing wind, and muffled sobs, I began to curse the perceived fabricated love my father had for me. See, this is why I don't do feelings. How could he get rid of me like this? *Man up, big boys don't cry.*

For hours along that drive, I told myself that my father didn't want me, and this was his way to enjoy the family as he desired it to be—him, my mother, and my sister. I was the defective toy that had no longer been useful. Or maybe my father was jealous of my manhood. Maybe he knew that I would soon become tougher, stronger, and better than him. Or better yet, he wasn't the man I had thought he was, and he was the man God knew he was.

You see, my father, that day, made a choice that would

forever change the dynamic of his family. Although I'm sure my parents spoke about their decision, it was on my father's plate to execute the directive. My father's words, in essence, ripping a mother from her child, becoming a target of vitriol to his only son, and more devastating, having to admit, as a man, that you failed to prepare your first boy for the world. What my father did that day, while challenging at the moment, was the greatest show of manhood I have ever seen.

We as men struggle to admit our faults, not because we can't be wrong but because it shows our fallibility. Sadly, in the mind of a juvenile David, all I saw was disloyalty. I was written off and thrown asunder. Under the impression that I no longer mattered to my father, I decided at that moment that in order to achieve the manhood my father wanted to keep me from me, I could never rely on another person again.

Just a few months into my incarceration, my family made the trip to the facility in which I resided. Excited at the chance to spend time with my family, I made haste to the space designated for visiting. Upon entrance to the visiting room, my insecurities began to flare at the sight of my mother. There my mother stood perfectly beautiful as she had always been, yet today, she had a glow. My mother was pregnant with a boy, nonetheless. Not only did they cast me away, but they replaced me. *Man up, big boys don't cry.*

After five rebellious months in prison, I was sent to a group home on the other side of the state. In this move, I was excited because it allowed me to get as far from the hurt of my family's betrayal as possible. While housed in the boys' home, I began to fabricate stories whenever asked about my family. They died in a car accident. They left me as a child; I am an orphan. All in efforts to hide the hurt I felt in their excitement of this child.

Until one day, I was informed by the staff that I had a day pass coming the following weekend; my dad would be coming to visit and taking me shopping. No longer able to hide behind my mask of forced manhood, I began to break down. Why would this man, who I professed hatred toward, drive hours just to come to spend money on me? After everything I'd done, how could he love me so?

Once again, the answer is simple. It is because he wasn't the man I thought he was; he was the man that God knew he was. My father loved me beyond my faults. He pushed away his own pride, his own prejudices, and his own focuses on being a man. He loved me enough to turn down his own "man" and just was my dad. Just as my dad did for me, God does for us every day, despite our professed displeasure with Him. While our manhood screams, "How dare He leave me?" God dares not to.

So often, we get caught in a loop of cognitive distortions causing us to conflate focused help with betrayal. Thus, leaving us in a state of paranoia, destined to ruin our lives before allowing anyone else to do it. We must get to a place where we stop being the man that we think we are and become the man God knows we are.

Whether you have/had a father in your life or not, God always has and will always be your Father in heaven unequivocally focused on your help, albeit sometimes not in the fashion in which you envisioned. Sometimes, you're going to get away with doing things on your own, causing a sense of machismo, but truth is, God is watching with interested eyes waiting to catch you when you ultimately fall.

While I can't be sure if my father ever felt as if he should disown me or write me off as a bad seed, I can be sure that my father never stopped fighting to show me what manhood really meant—simply loving your family so much so your manhood becomes obsolete. Pardon my digression but Dad, thank you for being the man that I always needed. Thank you for showing me just what God had planned. Thank you for being my dad.

Whew, now that I got that out, back to my story. The time finally came for my release from the group home. Unsure of my standing in my family structure, I boarded my father's vehicle to be whisked away to what I was sure to be a dungeon of depravity and contempt. Along the several hours of road trip, my father did as he always did and listened to his books on tape, focused on navigating the winding road of the mountain pass. I wonder if he knows how much I enjoy these times. Does he care that I, like him, love books but really could do without the reading part? I wonder if he remembers that we used to be best friends. Or does he even care now that they have the baby?

For hours my thoughts haunted my psyche, creating a mounting level of despair set only to the frequency of my own self-loathing. With every mile-marker passing, I became more and more aware of my inadequacies. By the time of arrival at my parents' home, I was in full-blown crises. *Man up, big boys don't cry.*

Uneased by the presence of what I could only qualify to be my replacement, I decided that my best course of action was to just accept the reality of my situation and become an afterthought, just as I was sure my family wanted me to be. Unable to ask for help, I reverted to what I knew best—manhood, or so I thought.

06 | BOYS DON'T MAKE MEN

Perched high upon my throne, it was bound to only be a matter of time before I must pay the cost of the crown.

I became so determined to eradicate emotion from my life, I began to jump from partner to partner, friend to friend, never truly allowing for a relationship to ever set in. Subsequently, the perceived betrayal of my family and loss of my best friend foreshadowed the direction in which every relationship I would come to have would end in my ultimate emasculation. Focused on not allowing for emotion was the only thing that made sense to me. I intently began to remove myself from the Jackson family equation, spending more time alone in my own solace or running the streets continuing my conquest of manhood.

Around this time, I was beginning to look like a man. Standing six foot three and two hundred and fifty pounds, I began to set my sights on older companions whom I believed would foster my manhood. After only a few months of daily activity on a popular social media site, I came across a young lady interested in the cultivation of said manhood.

While uniquely adapt to the courting process, I was less proficient at dealing with genuine feelings. For the first time in my life, I began to accumulate substantive feelings for a woman; the only issue was that she was four states away. This caused a problem for my immature mind to process. In relaying my concerns to my paramour, her only response was, "You can come live with me. I would love to have a man in the house." Exuberant at her acknowledgment of my being a man, I quickly acquiesced to her suggestion with minimal questions about the sustainability of her idea.

Over the next few days, I covertly prepared myself to begin my journey. Two days after Christmas, with the smells of the holidays still lingering in the air, under the cloak of darkness, I wrangled my luggage together, set to realize my destiny.

Five hours later, I found myself on a bus scheduled for a two-day ride with two-hour money. As previously stated, sustainability was never my concern, especially in matters of manhood. All that mattered to me was this young lady knew I was a man and offered a kingdom in which I could reign. After about fourteen hours of travel, nodding my head to whatever artist played through the portable CD player my father had given me just a few months before, I began to notice pronounced rumbles signifying my apparent hunger and need for sustenance.

Upon reaching the next scheduled break, I exited the bus heading straight to the makeshift store located within the bus terminal. Understanding the lack of money in which I processed, I began to attempt to identify an affordable fix to my agitated stomach. Quickly realizing that I could afford nothing more than a grossly inflated candy bar, I tucked my pride and walked out, hunger now exacerbated. As if God had a laugh track cued up to the sitcom of my life, I began to feel as if everybody in the little station was looking at me and laughing a silent heckle to themselves. *Man up, big boys don't cry.*

I would be derelict in my duties if I didn't take this opportunity to explain, if only to myself, that God is vehemently invested in the viewing of our lives. Our every scene, our every act, and our every commercial are prime for His viewing pleasure. Just as a sitcom, these productions have their ups and their downs, their comedy, their drama, and their tragedy. We must understand that God is inherently invested in your next episode. While He was the author and director of your story and knows what you were designed to do, there is still beauty in watching your beloved creation reach its apex. You are the Imago Dei, created in the very image of God. I'm sure God has yet to be laughed at. So, while at times you believe yourself to be God's punchline, understand you're made in His image, and He has the last laugh, so maybe you should laugh with Him.

Okay, now that I got that praise break-in, let me return you to the topic at hand. After boarding my bus and pulling off, I was soon roused out of my sleep by the sounds of a young woman soothing her babe with nurturing, hushed words. As if my glance carried weight, the young woman looked in my direction and begged my pardon for waking me from my sleep. Unsure of what to say, I quickly nodded in appreciation and gave her the best smile my delirium could muster. Assuming the conversation was over, I began to look out of the window quickly remembering the hunger that set in much earlier that evening.

After the aggressive rumbles of my stomach's angry disposition, the young woman asked if I was hungry. She had sandwiches that her mother made her and wouldn't want them to go bad before she could get to them. Aware of the hit that my perceived manhood could take if she was aware that I had no money, I hastily told her, "Oh, I got money. I just didn't see anything in the store that I liked." With a curious "Okay," she flipped, opened her bag, and handed me two sandwiches. Unable to hide my pronounced hunger, I began to eat the sandwiches with reckless abandon.

Once my meal had been laid to rest, I voiced my appreciation, only to be met with the peaceful snores of my new compatriot. Now, unable to recapture sleep myself, I looked at this young woman holding her baby with such care and longed for the days of safety in the arms of my mother. No longer was maternal nurture available to me; gone were the days of security in the presence of my father. Today I had to become a man. Well, at least by the time my convoy was due to arrive.

After several hours spent listening to glorified personifications of manhood delivered over a nice beat, I'd finally arrived at my desired locale. Anxiously, I bounded off the bus only to be met with the heat of an unforgiving sun and the emptiness of the unnervingly quiet terminal.

Once again, not worried about the sustainability of this idea, I called my damsel with hopes that she was just running late. Greeted by the excitement in her voice, she explained to me her inability to come to pick me up and that she needed me to ride the city bus to her location. And, not to worry, it would be a fairly quick ride. Unwilling to explain to her that I only possessed about two dollars in change, I spent my last on the actualization of the fallacy termed manhood.

Have you ever given your last to be deemed a man? While it may not always hold monetary value, we as men often trade large sums to reach a height of male sovereignty. We trade families for flings, careers for conditions, and salvation for sex—all in the name of male dominance. We must identity the societally tainted aspects of manhood and rid them from our working definition. We must recalibrate our moral compasses and understand that the cost of manhood should never out-weigh the cost of the blood Christ shed on Calvary.

Soon after separating from my last, I'd arrived at the front door of the kingdom in which I was soon to be crowned king. Once again, knocking at the door of a woman's house I had never met in person, I was greeted by the familiar face I had come to enjoy through pictures online.

Upon entering the home and settling in, I made sure to tamper any smiles that may have crested my face, intently set on the production of effective peacocking. As my plumage expanded, I quickly noticed the desired effects it was having on my partner. Within short array, things became physical, allowing me to display all that I had learned in the art of pleasure. Multiple partners and conquests, check. Proficiency in the art of pleasing a woman, check. Skilled in combat, check. Maybe, just maybe, I had finally become a man.

I rode the throne of manhood for a couple of months, never really becoming a man yet wearing the clothes and playing the role of one. Just as a minor child would play house on the playground, I was oblivious to the responsibility and nuances of manhood. Perched high upon my throne, it was bound to only be a matter of time before I must pay the cost of the crown.

Soon after taking reign of my new dominion, it was time for my first lesson in manhood's responsibilities. With the carelessness of a child, my companion hastily danced into the room, shouting for all to hear of her being with child. Unable to process the severity of our situation, I simply offered a "cool" and went back to whatever it is that I was doing. Offended by my nonchalant disposition, she quickly figured out that I was nothing more than a skilled imposter. Yet, what was she to do? She was now carrying a child believed to be mine. Within days, we were at a local free clinic in hopes of getting an ultrasound and sex determination of the child. "Congratulations! It's a boy," offered the ultrasound technician, unaware of my deficiencies in the space of manhood responsibilities.

Upon our exit from the facility, she simply looked at me

and shared her fear. Because at that moment, she, just as I, had realized that boys don't make men. How could I, as a boy myself, teach this child the ways of manhood? All the instruction of my father's manhood was muted by the lyrics of rap music and scripts of primetime television. I wasn't even man enough to be a father to my child. *Man up, big boys don't cry.* With all the pride I could muster, I told her we would be alright, that I got this. Unsure herself, she acquiesced to my position because, for neither one of us, was sustainability the dominant thought. You see, because she wanted a man and I looked like one, to her, that was enough to bet her existence.

We struggled through the next couple of months with me often missing meals to make sure she and the baby had enough nutrients to remain healthy. Upon collecting a windfall of money from an inheritance, she and I decided to move to the state in which I was from. To her, this was just a chance to be accepted into a family, and for me, it was more about me needing my father's guidance in raising a child.

Soon after our move back home, however, we quickly began to grow apart. Neither one of us truly appreciated nor understood the requirements of a relationship, allowing for instances of infidelity to permeate throughout the space. With every instance of cheating that I identified, my manhood began to become challenged. I began to become more aggressive, almost even violent, in my tones. I quickly reverted to the street life to which I had become so accustomed. Every found conversation became a texted threat to whomever she happened to be talking to. I never truly tried to create a relationship with my son because if she didn't see me as a man, how would he? Only after months of being in my home state, she packed her belongings and left citing fear of physical harm. Thus, the last time I saw the son believed to be my first-born child.

Unfortunately, I spent so much time purveying alpha masculinity that I didn't learn from that experience. You'd like to think that losing the opportunity to know my child would be a wake-up call, but no. My toxic thinking left space for me to fall prey to the same situation again, which I did.

07 | FRIEND ZONED

You must inherently be open to allowing for your vulnerabilities to be seen.

Panicked breaths streamed from my lungs in puffs of adrenaline-laced fear. The roar of gunfire echoed with the vibrance of a percussionist drum, booms announcing the opening of yet another stanza. Streams of a ruby red substance flow glistening in the streets, causing the amber hue of the streetlights to dance with grace and beauty. Unable to move, I stand still as swiftly moving projectiles tear through the fabric of the shirt I was wearing. I fall with a soft thud to the cold gravel of the road beneath me, simultaneously catching a glimpse of the person who caused my searing pain. As I lay there replaying the accolades of my adolescence, I began to place the face of the shooter. But how could that be? The shooter was me.

Suddenly, in a state of terror, I am jolted awake, sweating in attempts of escaping the fear-induced panic that befell me. Confused as to the meaning of my dream, I began to try and cleanse my mind of the fear that gripped me. *Man up, big boys don't cry.*

Over the next several months, varying iterations of this dream stalked the recesses of my slumber. It became so prevalent that I would stay awake until delirium in hopes of evading the terror sleep furnished. Forced insomnia became the diagnosis that defined my being. This sleeplessness became such a debilitating circumstance that I began to miss out on the things I enjoyed most due to my staying awake all night and sleeping only once critical mass had been achieved.

Can you see the irony of this parable thus far? Here I am, a boy devoutly focused on the destroying of my existence in aspirations of manhood yet running from a dream rooted in the scene of my own self-demise. Every day, my purpose and calling were being slaughtered by my own hand in the name of manhood, yet a dream paralyzed my sleeping pattern. What is more, I couldn't tell anybody of my sorted terrors in belief that my status would mark a sign of weakness within my subconscious masculinity. Night after night, forcing myself to stay awake, I continued to run, yet where can one run when God is the one chasing them?

Just as He did me, God has a divine purpose for every one of us. This purpose often becomes much maligned in our internal hierarchy of importance. Yet, it is truly the magnetic force that propels the needles of our moral compasses. My repeated dreams signified nothing more than a manifestation of my culpability in the derailment of my God-ordered purpose.

I began to conceptualize this theory soon after the departure of my most recent girlfriend and my child. In the grief of their exodus, I committed myself to growth, figuring maturation in manhood was sure to follow. With a new lease on life, I began to operate with some sense of direction. While the cultivation of manhood remained my dominant goal, education and spirituality quickly found residency within my aspirations.

Determined to redirect the trajectory in which I was traveling, I began to allow sports and academia to become my safe haven from the malicious intent of my own misguided thoughts. Within months, I was finishing school, set to explore the expanse of higher education. Because what's more grown-up than a college man? Yet, unable to fully put my toxicity behind me, I couldn't leave without first making sure the young lady that I had just met a few weeks previously knew I had my eyes on her.

Operating purely from a place of sexual conquest, I began to furnish this young lady with whatever elegant soliloquy I could in efforts to attain her attention. Only this time, something was different. My endearment-laced advances fell deaf on the ears of my desired companion. I was stifled by her abrasive disposition and matter-of-fact communication style. Posing a new challenge to my manhood, I began to become more elaborate in my courting—often telling her of my intended desires of a shared life together. I began to push so hard that soon the lines blurred. Thus, becoming less of conquest and more of a fixated desire.

As if by osmosis, maturation was beginning to breed manhood. I finally had identified the woman that I would spend my life with. Only she was not at all interested in me. Beaten back by the swell of insecurity growing within me, I forged on, only to be offered friendship. *Man up, big boys don't cry.*

Ever wonder why we as men believe it such a derogatory concept to be "friend-zoned"? We get so caught up in the title of a relationship we lose sight of its intended purpose. While friendships are often relegated to non-physical spaces, friendship uniquely allows for elevated emotional availability. Yet, emotional availability is deemed as a liability in the grand scheme of societally prescribed manhood. In order to be a friend, you must inherently be open to allowing for your vulnerabilities to be seen. Friendship depicts a portrait of trust wrapped in the free-flowing of information, yet we as men coward at the idea of ever trusting someone enough to even share our information.

While the "friend-zoned" dilemma most often shows itself in a relationship with the opposite sex, our lack of trust seems much more universal. Groups of men operate every day unaware of the effects of toxic masculinity that underline the lives of even their closest friends. More often interested in the glory stories of our pal's conquests, we rarely ask about that same pal's insecurities or, better yet, tell them ours. We have become so dissociated with emotions; we deem them to be merely humanistic realities rather than vital identifications of our overall self-understanding. We are taught that emotions breed weakness, therein eradicating any chance that we could begin to embrace them.

Being "friend-zoned" brought emotions, thus being unacceptable. Understanding this fact, I began to stage a full-court press in my courtship, often being met with comments such as "I don't want to mess up what we have" and "I just want us to get to know each other." Unrelenting in my pursuit, I spent the next calendar year stringing together uncountable amounts of fabricated lies to conquer this conquest, thus displaying my alpha masculinity.

Somewhere along my conquest, this friend no longer became a person but a mission—a trophy to win, a manifestation of my well-tuned male prowess. She was beautiful, could sing with the angels, and she could shout in heels. I was sure that my mother would like her. Yet, in the year of courtship, I never really took the time to do as she suggested and get to know her, thus causing us to mess up what we had.

I spent a year building a friendship with this young lady and never once told her how I truly felt. Everything came with a varying level of exposed peacock feathers attached. In the span of that year, three of my closest friends had been gunned down in separate acts of gang violence. Yet, all my manhood would allow me to share with her was how good she would look on my arm. Unaware of my broken pieces, she eventually acquiesced to my advances, thus cementing my belief in the importance of masculinity.

Within weeks of our agreed-upon relationship, I was over it; the challenge had been met—mission accomplished. Thus, making me acutely aware of the other challenges that existed elsewhere. I almost instantly created a pattern of cheating that lingered throughout the lifespan of our relationship. Operating completely unaware of my wrongdoings, my mate began to give herself fully into our space, creating an unbalanced environment.

Before my paramour could learn of my mistreatments, her emotions began to become unstable. So much so, a close friend of mine, after spending time around her, urged me to "get her checked." Allow me to interject into the story for just a moment. The phrase "get her checked" was an exact quote. I am sure that by now, you are beginning to see signs of toxic masculinity all around you. Sadly, upon hearing "get her checked," the level of toxicity that oozed from that phrasing alluded me. Unsure what to do with the varying level of emotions emitted from my partner, we believed in our archaic assumptions of there being a medical issue. Rather than ask what was wrong or if she was okay, we assumed she was broken and needed fixing.

Truth was, she simply was pregnant and needed me to stop pretending and be a man. Unsure of how to navigate this pregnancy, I decided to approach this one completely differently than I had before. Where I was absent before, I became laser-focused on being a part of every appointment, every ultrasound, and every milestone of my child's gestation. Yet, being there for my child couldn't supplant my lust for societal manhood. While I lavished the idea of being a father, I shuttered at the concept of monogamy. "The caged bird can't fly," is what

I told myself. Unaware that monogamy is the air that will lift you.

Throughout her pregnancy, I remained a constant fixture at her home. So much so, her mother allowed me to move in, completely going against her spiritual objections. Yet, for every hour spent rubbing the belly of my partner, there were thousands of text messages being shared with other "challenges."

Soon after the birth of my child, unsure of my life's direction, I began to ponder entrance into the military. Where better than to become a man than in the military? After spending time with a recruiter, I was told my entrance could only be approved if I did one of two things: get married or not have custody of my son. Unwilling to allow my son to be taken from me, I quickly shared with my mate the importance of getting married. Without sharing the motive behind my ask, she excitedly agreed, and within months, we were legally wed.

Once married, I quickly engaged the recruiter, to which I was told all that I needed to do was lose thirty-five pounds, and I would be a prime candidate for enlistment. Unable to motivate myself to lose the weight, I eventually brushed aside the idea, now feeling as though my marriage was for not. Operating under that belief, I began to conduct myself as if my marriage was nothing more than a farce that took more effort to end than it did to act like it didn't exist.

Unfortunately, toxic masculinity cares little about the people it tramples in its wake. She became nothing more than a cog used to turn the wheels of my manhood. Her feelings became arbitrary nuisances, often ignored in the achievement of my alpha masculinity. Sadly, I remained married to this young lady for four years yet moved out after about six months. Never once looking back to survey the damage which I caused. By any means, I would achieve manhood, regardless of who was in my way, even if it was me.

In not understanding the advantage of the "friend zone," I never truly learned to know my mate beyond the adventure of the chase in which she represented. Her hopes, fears, and dreams, all facts lost on my one-track mentality. Manhood was the goal, and she served as little more than my launchpad to greatness. What is more, I never allowed her to know the brokenness in which I existed. She never knew that my trauma wouldn't allow me to ask for help because experience told me that, when caught in honey, no matter how loud you scream for help, nobody will ever hear you. Even in a pool of your own blood, the only thing you can rely on is your own strength, so you better not be weak. She never knew that every time she mentioned another man, my hurt told me that I was replaceable because if my own mother could replace me, so could she. She never knew that my dreams told me that my death was coming and it would be by my own hand. She never knew that all I wanted to do was cry. *Man up, big boys don't cry.*

I miscalculated the healing that friendship represents. Due to my general fear of attachment by that time, I had only about five friendships in which I coveted. Yet, all were based on masculine pretenses forged out of the fire of gang warfare. In none of those relationships had I ever told someone of the anxiety I have when faced with emotions. With none of them did I share my broken pieces; none of them knew anything more than my affinities for violence and sexual conquest—the things I believed showed them my manhood.

We as men must get to a point where we seek meaningful friendships, where gone are the days of war stories and intimacy sagas, where our interactions are built on a foundation of collective emotional intelligence. We as men must unite in the dismantling of societal norms and begin to build up substance in its place.

I can remember in my early twenties, I was introduced to my brother-in-law (cutting out "in-law" from here—that's my brother!), whom I was told had been around for years, yet I never really paid attention enough to notice. He said something that, then, had a profound effect on my life. Before I get to that, let me tell you about my brother first. He is the complete opposite of me. Where manhood to me was defined in my outward appearance, he has always been an inward display of character. My brother, all six-foot-eight inches of him, would often be seen in tiny pink Bermuda shorts, silk V-neck t-shirts, and pink Ferragamo slippers. Oh, and please don't let me forget his Prada "man bag." Yet, he has shown me more about how to be a man than any other beyond my father.

For years, I would see my brother drive an hour beyond his

destination to pick my sister up for church, fully aware that he would have to take her back once service was over. For years, I watched him cater to my sister as if she was born on this earth solely for him to cherish. For years, I watched him outwork my father's example of how my sister should be loved. For years, I watched him emotionally avail himself to the foundation of love. Yet and still, this wasn't the most represent display of manhood I had come to see from him.

I can remember after being told of their upcoming nuptials; my aunt asked my brother where his bachelor party would be. Jokingly, he mentioned, "The library." As only my aunt could do, she explained to him that "strippers read, too." True to form, he laughed, agreed, and proceeded to host his bachelor party at a bowling alley with the entire family in attendance. Yet again, only a glimpse at his manhood.

The thing that caught me most about my brother is he loved himself enough to know he needed friends in which he could be emotional. Sometime in my early twenties, my sister was talking about a group in which my brother and his friends started that was focused on the fellowship and collaborative growth of its members. This group would meet every Monday night, coinciding with the football game with the hopes of not only enjoying sports but allowing for a space of vulnerability.

While I believed manhood to be acts of force, he knew it to be signs of love. Not only was his emotional availability important but that of his comrades as well. While I struggled to identify manhood, my brother lived. If only my toxic masculinity would've allowed me to ask for his assistance. But as I previously stated, help was a word I despised.

Friendship, the "zone," and other like terms, should be seen as a badge of honor. That someone believes in you so much so that they ascribe desire to your emotional availability. We must begin to uplift the men around us, building communities focused on the collective emotional stability of our culture. Begin to ask your friends about their emotional status. Let them know that not only do you care, but you empathize. Show them your scars, in essence, affirming that theirs aren't so bad. As my brother taught me, love yourself enough to be emotional with your friends. Enjoy the friend zone!

08 | TO PORTLAND WITH LOVE

*I simply hung my head, more disgusted with myself
than disappointed with her.*

Then I met the woman who would come to be my life. When I set my mind to write this book, I did so immensely afraid of getting to this chapter. While I have the talent of lacing words to set a scene, I doubt I will serve well in the description of this one. How do you begin to describe the systematic dismantling of your heart, your feelings, of your confidence? What guidebook explains how to lay your hurt bare for the world to see? Who is the expert studied in the art of expressed trauma? Who knows how to explain that their wedding vows were no more than well-placed fabrications? Pray, tell me why they didn't tell me that, beyond all my adversity, my wife would be my greatest abuser?

"I just had to be around that man." The words that

will forever echo in the hollows of my heart. With the precision of a sniper round, those words entered into my being only to become logged within my insecurities, words belonging to none other than my wife when asked about the affair in which she had just been discovered. With every syllable, my greatest fears were realized. In a lapse of judgment, I had allowed myself to fall victim to the trap of emotion, and as I believed, here I was, once again, emasculated. *Man up, big boys don't cry.*

Along this journey of my relationship with God, family, and toxic masculinity, we talked about a litany of topics, none having a more profound effect on my unhealthy relationship with manhood than this. I had become the very display of weakness that I had spent a lifetime attempting to avoid. Unable to escape the hurt in which maligned my days, my nights fell cold with a chill and loneliness only matched by the Arctic tundra. How could this be that my manhood met destruction at the hands of my greatest accomplishment?

"I just had to be around that man." I wonder if she knew that from the moment I met her, I wanted nothing more than to be that man. In the meeting of my wife, my ability to peacock under pressure was instantly challenged. Never before had I been brought to my figurative knees in awe of a woman's beauty. All of my built-up defenses becoming nothing more than rubble at her feet, in which she simply swayed over it and took hold of my heart. It was at the moment that I met my wife that I came to learn the existence of perfect imperfection. I understood that nobody is perfect but, she was perfect to me.

I wonder if she knew that at that moment, all of my hurt finally made sense. No man should be so lucky to end up with her, so they had to go through some things to earn it. My wife became a constant reminder of why manhood was so important because somehow, someway, I had to win her heart. I wonder if she knew.

At the time of my meeting my wife, I was fully operating in a space of dual existence. Gone were the days of my academic focus, and I had begun to revert to the streets in which I believed manhood to take residence. Yet, I had found my lost love for church and made sure that my weekday masquerade never impeded my weekend salvation. I had achieved an ef-fective balance, is what I told myself, willing to operate in a space of dual-consciousness. A double-minded man is unstable in all of his ways. I wonder if she knew.

Due to the distance which she and I shared between us, it took my having to take a train for us to enjoy our first date. For four hours, I sat on that train nervously awaiting the butterflies in which I come to relish when she invaded my thoughts. I can remember telling my wife not to be late because if she was, I would just go meet up with some other woman. I wonder if she knew that there would never be another woman, that I didn't want her to be late because every minute that she was late was another minute I wasn't in her presence.

As if life went back to playing its laugh track, I walked off the train to an empty station. Suddenly, the empty bus depot from before began to permeate my thoughts. Although this time I had money to buy my food, I was once again was left to ponder the sustainability of this idea. I wonder if she knew that her being late meant I was alone.

Upon her late arrival to the station, I began to level up my peacock to maximum foliage. Believing in every woman's desire to have a strong man, I put on the most commanding voice and look I could achieve and told her of my dissatisfaction. With the grace that only my wife could achieve, she simply smiled and asked if I wanted her to take me somewhere else. I wonder if she knew that at that moment, I could do nothing more to keep from fawning over her than to just look out of the window and hope the reflection didn't give away the presence of my smile.

Shortly after our first date, it had come to my attention of my wife's conversations with another man. Upon finding the evidence of the destroying messages, I could do nothing but slide down the wall in agony. Unable to catch hold of a regulated breathing pattern, I began to cement the belief in all of my insecurities. Pants of tear-laden breaths escaped my lungs, violently ripping through the fortified walls of my self-prescribed manhood. Yet again, I have been deemed replaceable.

Regardless of the physical pain, my body began to feel, shouts of "man up, big boys don't cry" rang with the vibrance of a stadium's applause. Feeling as if my masculinity had betrayed me, I simply hung my head, more disgusted with myself than disappointed with r if she knew.

Moments later, the commands in my head became a call to action, Man up! Big boys don't cry! I quickly recouped my bearings feeling, that there must be a show of alpha superiority. Only after text messaged threats to her beau of "Where you at, homie?" and "You gotta come run this fade" was I able to regain what I believed to be my driving force. Unsure of my now challenged dominance, I did what I knew best, project manhood. After hours of tense arguments, I made my way back home primed to obtain the conquests that I had foregone.

Days turning into weeks, weeks turning into months, conversations turned into conquests, and still, I couldn't begin to remove my wife's smile from my thoughts. I wonder if she knew that I loved her from the moment I saw her. I wonder if she knew that my heart was simply a vessel built to hold reverence for her. I wonder if she knew.

After months of licking my wounds, I began to devise a plan. Although my wife didn't love me as I did her, I would never allow my manhood to go undefended. My wife, being a proud member of a Black Greek Letter Organization. I decided I would go back to school in her city and pledge a fraternity that was closely linked with her sorority; some would even say they were Phirst Pham (the first family). Upon receiving acceptance into the school and interest of the fraternity, I packed my bags and set off to Portland with love.

Soon after my arrival, my wife and I began to forge something beautiful in its simplicity. While no real title was ever placed upon our romance, we functioned in a space of elevated friendship or however close toxic masculinity would allow me to get to it. With vows of "we see eye to eye," our future began to look like a masterpiece that could have only had divine architecture. Well, until you began to look below the surface of our shallow commitments.

I wonder if she knew that societal manhood doesn't promote monogamy or that I suffered from a chronic dose of the radiation of masculinities toxins. I wonder if she knew that I must avenge the remnants of my hurt. I wonder if she knew that with every day that passed, my insecurities began to multiply with the same effect of metastasizing cancer. Unable to ask for help, I began to sink within my manhood, becoming aloof and cut off from her emotional advances. Our story is marred by imperfections, but I wonder if she knew it was perfect for me.

Reality is no; she didn't know. There was no way for her to have known because I never told her. What my story didn't tell you was that my wife, at the beginning of our relationship, was looking for one thing in me, that being security. She wanted, not needed, to understand that her sustainability was my focus. That her safety was my focus. And while combat was something I excelled at, she needed emotional safety, which toxic masculinity breeds very little of. While she knew something was wrong, she didn't know what. While she knew I needed help, she didn't know how. While she knew I was broken, she didn't know when. While I wonder if she knew, I never stopped to wonder if I knew.

Manhood is a plague that has ravaged our generation. We tell these young women any manner of lies to cover the scars of our masculinity, hoping that between their legs, we can find the key to our purpose. Sex is nothing more than a form of communication created by God to be shared between two people He has placed within a relationship. Just as in a video game, in order to proceed to one level, you must first master the one before it. Yet, so often, we can describe her bedroom before she can describe our hurts. I wonder if I knew that I was broken. I wish I could say to you that soon after, I learned to tell my wife of my shortcomings. I wish I could say to you that she learned of my brokenness. I wish I could say she finally fell in love with me, yet I can't. *Man up, big boys don't cry.*

After months of operating under the guise of manhood, I began to notice the life that I was living measured up very little to the life that I wanted. While in a constant holding pattern with my wife, I began to speak to other women as it became more evident that she was interested in other guys. Adamant of my not being replaced, I simply removed myself from the equation—offering pseudo friendship and sporadic shows of intimacy.

Whenever asked by my wife what I wanted from her and what we were, I would deflect with "do you," hoping that she would just say out loud that I wasn't man enough to sustain her. Because if she just told me, I could at least stop pretending. With every passing day came a new text to her phone with some guy promising a life that I wanted nothing more than to give her, but she didn't know that my masculinity wouldn't let me.

Sadly, popular media indoctrinates young boys into perpetual states of what's called the "male gaze." Life is filmed through the lens of masculinity, dipped ego, and toxicity, often allowing no room for emotion-based concepts such as love and relationship. This does little more than alienate the feeling-based core of adolescents, thus causing the numbing of our emotional receptors. Due to this numbing, they offered her a love I couldn't even give her if I wanted to.

In response to this understanding, I began to force myself into places of compromised comfort. For once, I had found someone worth trading my manhood. Days began to pass, and she fell oblivious to my newfound tenacity. Nights spent watching movies on the couch always interrupted by her privacy postured texting. *Man up, big boys don't cry.*

After a conversation with her best friend, who happened to be my frat brother, I decided to allow myself one leap of faith. Unbeknownst to anyone around me, I began to devise my plan—marriage, that was the answer. How could she not know of my love if she could see a ring on her finger? How could she not know of my love if, for once in my life, I was prone on one knee in a sign of submission? I wonder if she knew.

Eventually, after saving for a few months to purchase her ring, I decided that I would propose on her birthday while sharing our customary birthday dinner. Unable to contrive a story that could garner her parents' phone numbers, I simply requested to use her calculator while she was beginning to fall asleep. Upon accessing the phone, I began to scroll down the text history in search of the desired contacts. Only instead of her family, I was met with her ex, in which she had recently said that he was the most amazing man she had ever met. Unable to catch my breath, I slammed down the phone and ran out of the room as if able to run away from the knowledge of that missive. If he was the most amazing man, then what was I? *Man up, big boys don't cry.*

Now aware of my standing in the hierarchy of my wife's desires, my insecurities began a full-blown assault on my self-worth. Within minutes I was in my car, driving aimlessly. Text messages souring through the ether at rapid speeds in hopes of solidifying someone to validate my worth. Maybe my manhood was enough for somebody. I wonder if she knew that I wanted to be that amazing man. Instead, here I was, speeding through the streets in search of purpose.

Sadly, my misguided manhood brought me to the door where validation is sold one singular dollar bill at a time—a strip club. After hours of machismo-building flirting, I decided that I needed to man up and that big boys don't cry, so the only logical choice was to move on to my next conquest. Days later, with plans to visit my son, I began the drive back to my hometown with eyes on possibly furnishing some of the connections I had made in the previous days.

Within my trip home, I spent much-needed time with my son while attempting to bed his mother; maybe she still knew I was a man. After being rebuffed as "playing around too much" and "I need to focus on my son," I quickly moved on, avoiding any and all unnecessary hits to my masculinity. Fixated on the conquering of yet another conquest, I began to reach through the bowels of my social media. I happened across a young lady that I had come to speak with a few times. Intrigued with her late-night profession, I sent a message in hopes that her lips dripped honey. For days my message went unanswered until on or about August 20th.

09 | ON OR ABOUT AUGUST 20TH

I spent the next couple of weeks riding the high of my latest conquest yet saddened by whom I had become.

When living a life guided by the concepts of toxic masculinity, one often finds themselves in positions of peril. Masculinity often impedes one from reaching not only the desired effect but divine purpose. In order to live the life that God called you to live, you must be who God called you to be. Unfortunately, when waiting on God to show us our purpose, we often become derailed in the mire of masculinity. Yet, it remains true that the only thing worse than waiting on God is wishing that you had.

It was in the space of wishing I had waited on God that I'd come to learn my greatest lesson. On or about August 20th, I received a text that, like any other day, was rooted in the foundation of sexual conquest and masculinity boosting pride. As previously stated, I messaged this young lady in hopes of exploring the taboo nature of her late-night profession. In my head, what better way to prove your manhood than to convince this young lady to forego her fee? The goal was to make her want me and not the money.

I was successful in my pursuit of manhood that night. In fully utilizing every tool manhood had furnished me, I was able to achieve my desired outcome. In an artful display of lying and manipulation, I sold this young woman a dream of stability and monetary provision. As my vehicle navigated the moon-soaked roadways of the I-5 Interstate Highway, I began to recall the previous techniques I'd come to learn in the process of procuring manhood.

"Man up" taught me that, by any means, I was to be a man, expected to reign with an iron fist and well-versed in the acquisition of female submission. Instability taught me that while God has called me to be of a certain caliber, I mustn't forget to evaluate myself through the lens of others. I soon after understood that my abuse was inevitable, and before I become the victim, I must become the aggressor. Honey became my motivation to always exude strength. The love of a father seemed muted in my self-assessment. Thus, forging my unwavering belief in never allowing myself to be replaced or alone. Boys don't make men, so I was sure never to be seen as a boy again. The absence of love in the friend zone led me to Portland, where devastation ravaged my masculinity. So, on or about August 20th, it would be known I was a man.

I find it almost comical how we, as men, allow our justifications to become our definitions. We get so ensnared in our own misguided beliefs we never seek to find clarity in them. In evaluating the lesson learned techniques of manhood, we simply accept our jaded understanding as truth without ever cross-checking our beliefs against the Word of God. The issue with manhood is most don't understand it, especially those creating the definition.

I, just as many others, bathed in the corrosive rays of masculinity's glow. On or about August 20th, I became a culmination of my life's deepest traumas. My manhood grew in its importance, thus causing this young woman's worth to become irrelevant. No longer was I the young man that preached to Power Rangers; I was now an old boy who intimidated and berated women in shows of strength. Hurt people hurt people, and I was in critical condition.

In fits of raised tones and broken pride, I began to speak a language I was never taught. This language of aggression and pain began to formulate a dictionary of masculinity's making. "Just do what I say" became a common rationale, thus depicting my actions on or about August 20th. Because on that day, I was who I thought I was and not who God knew I was.

After reaching my goal of foregone fees, I, just as many other times in my life, quickly became disinterested. My belief was that I had achieved masculinity's apex, thus no longer in need of my late-night companion. Now operating under this new set of self-serving ideals, I quickly devised a plan to separate myself from the situation. Offering up a false story about a friend that was going to allow her to stay with them, I left her standing at the locked door of an apartment and drove away, disgusted with whom it is that I had become.

You know, for a person who never wanted to be alone, I struggled around people—mostly that of the opposite sex. You see, because women were the only ones that could invalidate my manhood, if I stayed around too long, they would become aware of my inadequacies. If I had allowed her to stay with me, she would see that I lived in a tiny bedroom with three other roommates. She would realize I was driving a rental car. She would come to learn of my lack of money to afford cable or internet connection. If I had allowed her to stay with me, she would see that my fear of judgment was only outmatched by my fear of emasculation. *Man up, big boys don't cry.*

As if my man battery had been recharged, I spent the next couple of weeks riding the high of my latest conquest yet saddened by whom I had become. Duality began to destroy me from the inside out, ravaging the inner workings of my emotions. The truth was, no matter my actions on August 20th, I couldn't seem to erase all the hurt that my life had come to amass. Operating in spaces of so-called masculinity, I did nothing more than further decimate the lining of my emotions. I knew I wanted more for my life, but masculinity wouldn't ever let me have it.

Upon sensing the raging war of factions within my soul, I began to focus on the activities in which brought me peace— church and academia. After months of focused concentration in the aforementioned areas, things began to look up. Academically, I began to live up to the potential most saw in me while simultaneously bolstering my presence at Sunday service. I was committed to defeating the enemy that lay dormant within my insecurities. Yet, how do you defeat an enemy that you won't even acknowledge exists, an enemy that you refuse to see?

While I was supposedly doing well and focusing academically, every night came with a new text inquiring about some young lady's late-night availability. Church became nothing more than an elaborate fashion-centric speed dating circuit. With the finesse of a used car salesman, I bounced from woman to woman, sharing embraces uniquely aware of who's embrace was held for an elevated time.

Under the guise of being an eligible bachelor, I stalked the carpeted hunting ground with the stealth of a lion, mighty in the efforts of my pursuit, unaware of the growing frustration that God was beginning to build with me. Truth is, it's not that I was unaware; I just didn't care. I was going to do this my way. I was a man and deserved the spoils of my dominion.

I believed this or some variation of it until one day while visiting my parents. I left their home only to walk directly into the surprised faces of two US Marshalls. Curious as to their reasoning for being there, I asked what they needed, only to be met with a simple command that seemed so very familiar, "Please, put your hands behind your back."

Certain that this was a misunderstanding of some fashion, I inquired to the reasoning of my arrest, only to be told that things would be explained to me once I reached the jail in which had jurisdiction over my case. Becoming growingly alarmed at my situation, I began to reach into my forgotten bag of tools and did something that seemed foreign to me at that moment—I began to pray.

Prayer is such a powerful tool. A tool in which could open any door, drill any hole or build any building, Yet, when used only in the time of need, often becomes obsolete. Prayer is simply the foundation in which relationship with God is constructed. If the foundation doesn't exist, how could one even begin to believe they could utilize the space? Often becoming so engrossed in our own masculinity, we believe vulnerability, even with God, poses a threat, only reaching a position of contrite relationship when in need—pulling out prayer with the intention of using it as an ATM and withdrawing needed blessing believed to have been stocked up from prior past good.

We become so fixated on the production of masculinity we forget that time with God must be intimate. And if one desires intimacy, they must first begin to turn their man levels down, allowing God the requisite space needed to begin pouring the foundations of relationship. Yet, before this can take place, we must not only be aware of toxic masculinity, but we must be truly focused on the expansion of our emotional reservoirs. So, while I offered my prayers, I did so on an altar of dulled emotions because I wasn't circumventing my manhood for anybody, not even God.

As you would assume, this left me feeling lonely and afraid. Here I stood, incarcerated for a crime that I had yet to identify, praying to a God I had yet to commit to, in need of a love that I had yet to man down for, all the while telling myself to *Man up, big boys don't cry.* Unknowingly, that day began my exodus to my very own wilderness.

After hours of being transported from jurisdiction to jurisdiction, I finally reached my destination. Not new to the justice system, I looked at this as just another insistence in which I would serve a few days and leave before anybody ever began to question my disappearance. Noticing the eyes of the others being herded through the booking system, I began to expand my feathers in preparation for a masterclass on peacocking. Within minutes of me shooting some unsuspecting gentleman across the room my manliest of glares, I was called to the desk to begin my processing.

Mere moments after taking the obligatory photograph and having my fingerprints placed on an electronic file, I was ordered to begin the walk to my holding cell. Still operating with the understanding that this would be a minor cause, I inquired of the charge in which I was being held. Upon reaching the door to my cell, the guard looked at me and simply said, "Rape." The door slammed shut with a violent thud that shook me to my core. As the dark room began to grow colder, I sunk down the wall of the concrete room, contemplating the words of the officer. Rape? How could this be? They must have the wrong man. Real men don't need to take sex; they are offered it. They must know that. *Man up, big boys don't cry.*

Unable to calm my nerves, my breath began to escape the

control of its typical cadence. Sweat dripped from my brow, carving a path down my cheeks for the tears that refused to follow. Pain radiated through my chest with the concussive pressure of a loaded cannon, crushing my sensibilities with every passing minute. Ultimately, an overcompensating dose of masculinity coursed throughout my body, pleading with my emotions to cease and desist. Weakness was an unwelcomed sight within the eye of manhood, thus not allowed for any reasoning. *Man up, big boys don't cry.*

After days of fear, riddled panic, I was released from the county jail on bail, intent on putting this nightmare behind me. Unaware of the presence of a reporter at my bail proceedings, I got back to my cellphone only to be greeted with texts asking about the authenticity of an article posted in the local newspaper. I immediately began to curse God for the role He had to play in my humiliation.

How could He do this to me? I prayed to Him sometimes. I went to church every Sunday, making sure to praise Him between my admiration of the female churchgoers. And I even made sure to use His name when telling the same young ladies that God told me that we should be together. What is more, I even knew enough Bible to twist it in my favor. How could He possibly leave me stranded in this place of misery?

My manhood told me that I needed nobody but myself, yet God was more interested in my denying myself. In that season, I was given an opportunity to cast aside the broken ways of my youth and look to build a true relationship with the Lord.

Sadly, my man-up mentality didn't allow for such concepts.

For several months after my being arrested, I operated in an elevated state of masculinity. How dare the criminal justice system tarnish my societal reputation? Every promise made to the Lord from the confines of that cold dark dungeon was quickly replaced with stereotypical acts of old. No longer in need of my divine ATM card, I put it away only to be used again in my next time of need.

That time of need quickly manifested when notified by my attorney that my trial would begin the following week. After months of pretending like this day would never come, I now had to fight for my freedom. Four days of trial and jury deliberation couldn't seem to shake loose the pressure-building storage of my masculinity-laced emotions. While my wife stood diligently by my side, I couldn't even allow her to see my fear. Possibly, if I showed her I was strong through this, maybe I would one day be the most amazing man she had ever met. *Man up, big boys don't cry.*

After a pause that seemed to span an eternity, the judge began to read the sheet of paper supplied to him by the jury. Moments later, I looked to my wife, who sat there crying as my father solemnly nodded his head, telling her that everything would be okay and that if one person's life was changed by my story, then it was all worth it. Man up, big boys don't cry, but how do you not cry after hearing "guilty"?

10 | 6 1/2 TO LIFE

Men only respect men, yet ironically, prisons often are overrun with boys.

Guilty. A simple word that set to motion the production of chaos that engulfed my psyche. With that singular word, my freedom was taken only to be outdone by the growing reminder of emasculation that defined the criminal justice system. Regardless of my physical strength and cardiovascular fortitude, my manhood was no match for the emotional weight of my current disposition. To the growing shouts of "man up, big boys don't cry," I began to give up. There couldn't be a God because if there was, how could He do this to me? *Man up, big boys don't cry.*

After the first night of my being a convicted felon, I began to bargain with God.

"Lord, if you allow them to take this back, I won't curse again."

"If you allow me to win on appeal, I will get saved."

"If you show me your love, I'll tell the world of your goodness."

"Please, God, if I have to do this time, allow my wife to stay by my side. I just can't lose her."

Just as I had assumed would happen, God never answered, or so I thought.

With every passing minute of my incarceration, the concept of control began to slip out of my needing grasp. Unable to establish my male prowess through any other means than violence, I soon reverted to what pieces of masculinity that jail allowed me. The only thing keeping my mind hopeful for a brighter tomorrow was the idea that my wife would take the journey with me.

Set on this need, I found myself, prison-controlled payphone in hand, pushing the requisite buttons to reach the voice in which I craved. With an uncoordinated sequence of words, I shared with my wife her importance in my life, ending the phone call with a proposal that left much to be desired to her childhood fantasies. Regardless of my proposal's shortcomings, she quickly obliged my request with an assurance of her loyalty to me and desire to move forward in matrimony.

With a newfound excitement, I went into my sentencing hearing, sure that God would intervene to my satisfaction. I was always told that He would never put more on me than I can bear, and prison was entirely too heavy for my liking. Refreshing my previous promises of changed behavior, I braced for the impact of the judge's discretion. Unwilling to accept the prosecution's harsh sentence, the judge explained to me the limitations set forth due to our state's mandatory minimums for such crimes. The judge went on to explain that regardless of his own desires, the least he could sentence me to was seventy-eight months to life. *Man up, big boys don't cry.*

Unable to focus enough to calculate the months into years, I simply nodded my head, stuck out my chest, and allowed my emotions to become numb to the shock of my current situation. Moments later, while being ushered out of the courtroom, I stole a glance at my new fiancée, sure that her love was the only thing I had left because God had forgotten about me. If only I would have known that God was still there and her tears were nothing more than a veil to cover the stains of the previous weekend's infidelities.

In that instant, I began to love my wife more than I loved God; she was still here, and He had deserted me. Looking back at my life, this happened to be my biggest recurring issue. Regardless of the trauma faced, the gang banging, or the toxic masculinity, my issues most always resulted in the same outcome—my loving the moment over He who created the moment. I felt as though because God allowed my suffering, He couldn't have loved me. Yet, I never attributed God the growth that always followed that very same suffering. Just as pressure is used to forge diamonds, it was imperative that I be pressure rated at the highest levels in order to achieve all that God had designed for me.

Sadly, this perspective escaped me for the next several months. Thereafter I began to operate in a space of self-reliance. Only taking breaks to level set with my soon-to-be bride, completely unaware of her accumulating infidelities. It was in this space that manhood's definition began to morph, if only just a little bit. I began to define the worth of a man by the level of loyalty he could garner from his wife. Unknowingly walking myself into yet another position of emasculation. She was spending the money needed to converse and often made sure my hygienic needs were met, so surely, she was aware of my ever-present manhood even if the DOC system was not.

Soon after my transfer from the county jail to the state prison system, I was thrust headlong into a cauldron of broken men looking to parade their masculinity through various acts of peacocking. Each cell laying claim to yet another fabricated facade made up of ignored emotions and elevated toxicity. It took only days in this cement arena before anger began to course through my body, eradicating any sign of hope that I may have held. Hope was a dangerous emotion because hope breeds vulnerability.

Unsure if I knew this then or if I began to learn this over time, but within these concrete walls and barbed wire fences, vulnerabilities soaked the tiered walkways. Each scowl, each puffed-up walk, each elevated vocal tone, all displays of masculine vulnerability. Each night, broken men are herded into their cells with commands of "Cell in now," realizing they have no greater claim to their lives than cattle. Which is more, their cells often being the only place of solace, at night become lockboxes caging one in with their greatest fear—emotions.

Unable to hide from your emotions, and often being with-out any stimulant to capture your thought, the cell begins to build pressure exacerbating any traumatic wounds that may lay dormant just below the surface. If one were to listen close-ly, the sounds of silent screams would echo throughout the facility, accompanied by thuds of discarded costumes worn to establish an effective masculine production.

Yet sadly, the emotional warfare waged within the cells often seems much more terrifying than the violent repercus-sions of masculinities dramatic displays. Aggression in pris-on is respected, while emotions mark the defining factors of weakness. Prison teaches that by any means necessary, one must not allow weakness residency within themselves, often making one susceptible to predatory abuse. In protecting your-self from said abuse, you must show a mastery level proficien-cy in the study of masculinity because men only respect men, yet ironically, prisons often are overrun with boys. Thus, the quandary most find themselves in.

They were sent to prison in efforts of rehabilitation yet, more often than not, become more brazen in their masculine portrayals. In order for rehabilitation to take hold, one must be open to empathy, an emotion that often falls short on the numb tips of incarcerated fingers, causing bouts of confusion due to internal questions of "Why should I have remorse for someone else when nobody has remorse for me?"

Muted pleas for help hover over the dark cells with the dim glow of a streetlight. Unable to find their way through the darkness of their emotional deficit, these men operate blindly, using the sounds of aggression as a guide. Often becoming lost in masculinity's toxic reserves, these men become just another causality of purposeless living.

I, just as many others, have fallen victim to the penitentiary state of mind. Answering frustration with outbursts, fear with violence, and hope with disbelief. The department of corrections took away my future, or so I believed, until about the third year of my incarnation when I realized that God had specific need of my skillset and testimony. Although the courts believed they needed jurisdiction over me for six and a half years, God needed jurisdiction for eternity.

You see, my stumble made me humble. In prison, the term for one's incarceration is commonly referred to as their "fall," yet for me, I believe my incarceration wasn't a fall but a God-orchestrated stumble. I can remember my mother telling me that shortly after my incarceration, a prophetess from her church explained to her that God had need of me and needed to sit me down. If it wasn't for prison, I would have probably been dead before the marked ending of my sentence. *Man up, big boys don't cry.*

Subsequently, I began to take inward inventory of my life, evaluating the steps that led me to my current set of circumstances. Realizing that my choices weren't mine and that I did nothing more than accept the indoctrination of society's felonious ideals. Before the date of my birth, as a black male, statistics told me that my going to prison was nothing more than a sadistic game of Duck Duck Goose. Understanding this trending, I began to become obsessed with breaking the curve.

Day and night, I meditated on the roots of my stumble, looking for the lesson that I was to learn. Yet, it seemed the more I searched for God's guidance, the more I got lost. Unable to process the holding pattern in which God had me, I began to set out on my own forcing purpose in places that weren't meant for me. Maybe I was called to be a scholar. So, I took every educational opportunity afforded to me through the prison system, making vehemently sure to collect 4.0s along the way.

With multiple degrees now in hand, I still felt unsure of my role in the Master's plan. I began to look closer at my trauma, understanding that most of my hurts had never been said out loud. So, I began to talk to those around me, quickly learning of their need to talk almost as much, if not more, than I did. These men were in pain, looking for something to soothe the fire in which ragged within their broken beings. The criminal justice system told them that they were monsters, and society told them that they were defective. Sadly, for many of them, I was the first to tell them that they mattered.

While I was questioning God's love by placing me here, it was in this season that I began to be equipped with the tools of my purposed trade. You see, because it is in your wilderness that you will begin to gain a perspective that you wouldn't have gained any other way. In your stumble, you will find humility which diametrically opposes the precepts of masculinity which prepares you for eternity. It took prison to break my chains.

Understanding the need for the chain breaking of others, I began to mount an assault on the poisonous teachings of societal creation. Focusing on the successful reentry of the prison population not as ex-cons but as men. While lecturing against the very ideals of masculinity and unlocking people's knowledge of their possible covert depression, feverishly, I began dismantling the hold of masculinity's effects.

Yet and still, purpose had not been fully defined in my life. While I had identified symptoms of my calling, I'd yet to locate the root. In the exploration of my talents, I realized possibly that my way with words was meant for much more than for the conquest of women and better suited for the advancement of men within the kingdom of God. Now armed with this newfound revelation, I began to mesh it with some of my other talents and realized that seminary could go far in preparing me for this endeavor.

Soon after sharing my revelations with my family, I was enrolled in a correspondence Bible college with the plans of quickly achieving my degree. After a few courses, my excitement began to dissipate, causing me to question if I had understood the direction in which God was sending me. I truly believed that God was calling me to preach and share a message that would rejuvenate the men of our generation, yet I couldn't stick to my theological training for more than half a year. Maybe this wasn't my calling.

It wasn't that it wasn't my calling; it was because I went before I was sent. While in prison, I learned of the Greek word, *Kairos*, or God's time. So often, we as men desire to champion whatever task we are attempting, leading to our moving on if we are less than proficient. We must begin to understand that everything God has for you will be given to you in God's appointed time. While King David was called to be a leader, he must first be a shepherd. Before Moses could liberate his people, he was called to be an orphan. Before Joseph could save a nation, he was called to be a prisoner. And I couldn't have been a preacher before I began to heal.

I have found that in the season of healing, one must be prepared for more hurt. The closer one gets to their calling, the more dangerous they become to the adversary. Thus, the need for a stronger attack plan. Things seem to be going great for you when you live outside of the will of God because, essentially, you do not pose a threat. Yet within your Job season, when you seem to be fighting more and more to find the face of God, your hurt begins to pile up. It is in this place that you must ask yourself, "What is the true cost of living one more day outside of your purpose?"

11 | MY GREATEST ACCOMPLISHMENT

It is vital that we begin to prioritize reconciliation over revenge.

Forgiveness. Another one of those words that we all under-stand yet struggle to define. It was in the pursuit of heal-ing from the effects of masculinity that I would come to learn of the complications that forgiveness posed. Although vital to the detoxification of our thought processes, forgiveness often comes at a heavily traumatic price.

So often, we get caught in the particulars of forgiving and forgetting that we seem to miss the underline issue—we're hurting. Placing focus on another party for their offenses al-lows the opportunity for us to cover the pain of our trauma-tized emotional state. Consequently, we become so transfixed on the perpetrator of the hurt, never taking time to deal with the hurt itself.

It was in the progression of my healing that I would come to meet the restorative nature of forgiveness. Soon after the identification of my purpose, I was transferred to another pris-on facility. Still riding the high of my recent wedding ceremony, I was excited to be moving closer in proximity to my new bride. Unfortunately, I was unaware of the impending devastation that would meet me at my new home.

About a month into my residency at the new locale, I was introduced to a young man who was in dire need of an emotional release. After hours spent on the yard hearing of his tumultuous relationship with his cheating wife, I began to recognize a lot of his described warning signs. Coincidentally, those had been some of the very things I had noticed in my own young marriage.

Now curious as to the status of my wife's devotions, I called her, explaining to her I was aware of something and if there was anything she needed to tell me. After some feeble attempts at pacification, she soon began to explain to me the depths of her deception. Man up, big boys don't cry.

It was in this explanation of her deception that masculinity's grip on me began to reactivate. It was here that I learned that her fidelities were never in alignment with mine. That yet again, this woman that I had come to cherish thought me replaceable. "I just had to be around that man," were the words that came to echo throughout the chambers of my heart. I wonder if she knew that I needed her?

Soon after the initial shock and anger dissipated, I began to dwell within the ideals of toxic masculinity. Allowing anger to become my North Star, corrupting the accuracy of my moral compass. Forgiveness, at that stage, becoming simply unacceptable. This behavior could not and would not go un-punished. Yet, the only person that my masculinity punished was myself.

In the upcoming months, I would come to lose sight of my intended calling, trading clarity for the chaos that illustrated my emasculation. Drowning in the pain of betrayal only coming up for toxin-laced breaths of masculinity. I became so quick to condemn the growing emotion that I didn't even recognize why I was sent the emotion. There was something here for me that I could only get in this space.

It was in this dark, desolate space that I learned to fall on my face before God and do nothing more than cry. There was no fancy prayer, no elaborate cadence of melodic hymns, just tears. It was in the dark that I began to seek the light. For the first time in my over thirty years of life, I began to weep with no conscious thought of who may bear witness.

Yet and still, forgiveness alluded me. Unable to escape the fabricated images of my wife's escapades, I began to contemplate divorce. After multiple nights of stress-riddled insomnia, I found myself sitting before divorce papers, pen in hand. "This could not go unpunished," is what masculinity told me as I navigated the fill-in-the-blank document.

Understanding God's views on divorce, I began to seek the counsel of a mentor which I had come to work with in the ministry. Being sure to expose all of my wife's wrongdoing while conspicuously covering my own battle with toxic masculinity, his response took me by surprise. With a knowing glance and a look over the rim of his prison-issued reading glasses, he simply posed a single question, "Would you ever forgive yourself for not forgiving her?" Admittedly, the answer is no. Yet, my pride was more concerned with the optics of allowing her actions to go unpunished.

Often, my wife would tell me that I was more concerned with revenge than reconciliation, and at times, that sentiment rang true. Although to my jaded and broken pride, that statement seemed nothing more than the pleads of one who didn't want to have to carry the weight of their offenses.

Let's examine that statement for a moment: reconciliation takes concerted effort while revenge most often seems an automatic response. As with most anything else, we as men relish the immediate, thus causing our propensity for reflexive responses. Although the sweat equity of reconciliation is much greater, the bounty of such work is plentiful. Yet, to achieve the spoils of reconciliation, we must begin the comprehensive work of forgiveness. Subsequently, before we can tackle the concept of revenge and reconciliation, we must take a look at how forgiveness can not only be achieved but maintained.

Understand, I am by no means a scholar in the field of forgiveness; I simply am well versed in the need for and need to embrace forgiveness. In the search for effective forgiveness practices, we as men must first begin to change the gaze in which we decide to view the person of needed forgiveness.

Through the lens of masculinity, we cannot help but filter all interaction with varying levels of pride. It is in this pride that we become immensely aware, if not all together fixated on, of the optics of our situation through viewers' consumption. Toxic masculinity tells us that a man should be a man at all times, especially when people are looking. Forgiveness breeds reconciliation, while revenge defines masculinity.

In efforts to obtain true forgiveness, we must first shed the corrosive effects of the masculine gaze. No longer allowing ourselves to be controlled by the perception of others but guiding our broken relationships with reconciliatory ideals. When broaching the broken pieces of a tattered relationship, we must keep our minds on the collective goal of reinvigorated purpose. There was something that you and that person were meant to achieve, and that must become the focus, thus maligning the impact of the perpetrated hurt.

Understandably this concept is often easier to speak of than to put into practice. After the subjugation of constant masculine propaganda, we are, in essence, programmed to believe that the only acceptable response to wrongdoing is wrongdoing. Yet, it is in both the identification and the rectification of this folly that we can begin to abate the misteaching of masculinity's philosophies.

Once we have adjusted for the falsities of our thinking patterns, we can begin to start the actual work of forgiveness. Admittedly, the advancement of this ideal took me almost two years when challenged by the infidelity of my bride. Underlin-

ing the fact that in no stretch of the imagination is this trans-
formation easy.

In the ascertainment of forgiveness, secondly, we must recalibrate our moral compass to fall in line with God's divine
plan. No meeting is by chance. When we begin to understand
that all encounters have purpose, it allows us to look beyond
the fault of the person to the lesson they are there to demon-
strate. It is in this phase of understanding that purpose most
assuredly is elevated. With each opportunity for growth, there
is a coalescent equipping of skill needed to become effective
within your calling.

Lastly, when looking to achieve de-masculinization
through the redemptive work of forgiveness, said forgiveness
must be finite. Often getting caught in the distorted thinking
pattern of scorekeeping, we as men struggle to let something
go without making it known that the subject of our forgiveness
is herein indebted to us. This need to keep score manifests itself often once we feel as if the person in which owes us this
debt has begun to gain ground. Masculinity preaches that it is
imperative that we always be "up one" on whomever we are
dealing with. While simultaneously covering our own need for
forgiveness.

It was in this stage of forgiveness that my wife taught me
the importance of assuming positive intent. Societal teachings
have engrained into our belief that "Once a cheater, always
a cheater." Monikers like this become the truth in which we
challenge our relationships. In the assumption of positive in-

tent, I was able to begin to look at my mate's cheating as an instance and not an operating algorithm in which she was programmed to follow.

Assuming positive intent allows for disruption to land on the perch of logical thought. Affording opportunity for rational decisions under less than stellar circumstances. Only through the assumption of positive intent can forgiveness become finite, birthing trust into a once devastated space. It is here that reconciliation resides. It wasn't until I began to view my wife through the lens of positive intent that we were able to begin to reshape the foundation of our new relationship. I say new relationship because although we were the same people in the same marriage, it was forgiveness that gave us new purpose.

While I must admit there are moments of excoriated emotion in the random thought of my wife's wrongdoings, which is greater is the love masculinity did its very best to keep me from achieving. The truth of the matter is that forgiveness is hard and often a start-and-stop process that we must continue to wade our way through. Often in the pursuit of forgiveness, we will find ourselves pushed into spaces of heightened emotional surges, in which we must be diligent to not only accept but embrace. It is in the adaptation of emotional intelligence that we can begin to redefine masculinity, thus dislodging the effects of its toxicity.

Although the practice of forgiveness is taxing, it is in the finality of forgiveness that I have begun to heal. Almost instantly, the moment I allowed for forgiveness to be a complete process and not a ticking clock waiting to go off, I was able to move forward in the reunification of my marriage. Undoubtedly, after extreme levels of trauma, there will quite possibly be a lifetime of heightened awareness. Yet, we mustn't allow this awareness to become the beacon we follow.

Now, understand in no way, shape, or form am I advocating for you to continuously put yourself in positions of abuse. While reconciliation is the overall goal, we must always challenge its purpose against God's will. Some situations were not meant for you to stay in but for you to learn and move on, all the while forgiving any transgressions that may have occurred. Once again, easier said than done; I agree.

Masculinity has furnished us with a mindset that is vehemently opposed to forgiveness without some form of repercussion. It is the disillusionment of this ideal that we must break ourselves of. It is vital that we begin to prioritize reconciliation over revenge. Thus, allowing the opportunity for our healing to occur.

Now, let me reassure you that the implementation of forgiveness practices will challenge you, and you will undoubtedly fail your first couple of attempts. Yet, if you continue to place focused effort into this skill set, you will achieve the desired outcome.

Once again, I repeat, I am by no means an expert in the study of forgiveness, but in the reunification of my marriage, I have become quite proficient at the chore. The truth is I love my wife and have loved her from the moment I first saw her. Unfortunately, I was so entrenched in the studies of toxic masculinity that I was unable to share with her my feelings for fear of how I may be perceived. If only masculinity had allowed me to share with her the trauma of my youth in which birthed a collection of insecurities deep within my unsettled soul. Yet, while unable to change the past, forgiveness has allowed my wife and me to create a new future.

To learn the power of forgiveness is quintessentially the most imperative piece to the de-masculinization process. It is in forgiveness that we can finally begin to "man down." This chapter was titled "My Greatest Accomplishment" because it was in the learning of forgiveness that I truly began to meet happiness. I often inform my wife that she is my greatest accomplishment, not only because she let a broken man like me marry her, but she was the most vital component of my ability to man down.

12 | MAN DOWN

What is one more moment chasing the fruits of masculinity costing me?

It is believed that Frederick Douglas once said that "It is easier to repair strong children than it is to fix broken men." Reality is, almost anything is easier than repairing the broken pieces of our toxicity-ravaged psyches. Too often, we marry emotions to weakness, not allowing space for adequate emotional release, thus causing buildup leading to catastrophic failure. It is vital that we begin the process of detoxification. We must choose to no longer define our manhood through the lens of society but more through the value we impart to those around us.

The question we must begin to ask ourselves is: what is one more moment of chasing the fruits of masculinity costing me? What resources or psychological/emotional capital am I consuming when engaged in this practice? I can remember taking an economics class and listening to the professor as he explained to us the concept of there being "no free lunch." That somebody has to pay because all resources are owned and numbered, and due to that numbering, resources are scarce.

Brothers, your emotions are not arbitrary nuances to be ignored and discarded. Moreover, they are numbered resources paid with the blood Christ shed on Calvary. It was for your fear He was whipped. For your sorrow, He was spit on. For your anger, He was hanged. For your happiness, He died. For your victory, He rose. So, while emotions oftentimes seem fleeting, maybe even annoying, there is no free lunch.

There is a concept known to economists as "opportunity costs," which is just a fancy way of saying the ability to obtain any more of one thing; we must forgo the opportunity of getting the next best thing. Subsequently, it is the cost of opportunity that we, as men, often ignore. Headlong we run into perceived masculinity without ever checking the cost. Once again, I must pose the question: what is one more moment chasing the fruits of masculinity costing me?

My professor continued his lecture and went on to introduce us to how these opportunity costs are navigated. You see, through an economic perspective called "purposeful behavior," we equip ourselves with self-interested values. Purposeful behavior simply means that we make our decision with some desired outcome in mind. Due to this self-invested interest component of purposeful behavior, individuals look for and pursue opportunities to increase their utility. In other words—pleasure, happiness, or satisfaction obtained from consuming a good or service.

So, then in understanding how one begins to detoxify, we must ask ourselves: what added utility do we gain from operating in spaces of masculinity? What utility are you looking to increase in the achievement of societally defined manhood? Sadly, most of us cannot, or worse, refuse to identify what need we are looking to meet when in the thralls of misguided masculine performances. We get so caught up in the theatrics of our generational scripted roles that we fall blind to the purposeful behavior in which our utility is met. What are the costs of one more moment of chasing the fruits of masculinity? It is in the identification of our inner-most needs that we can begin to reverse the effects of our trained dispositions.

Throughout this journey, I have shared with you many of my most coveted displays of what I believed to be masculinity. Yet, unknowingly, I left you without the best part, the need in which I sacrificed my innocence to meet. For me, the need was simple, yet for years I was consumed with the inability of being able to voice it. All the while operating, unable to identify the need which I was trying to fulfill. How, per se, can I then expect my behavior to be purposeful? I, just like many young men, walked through life never able to say, "I just want someone to tell me they love me and mean it."

It is due to masculinity that my purpose became hidden. My behavior became erratic, never truly grasping the fundamental art of emotional intelligence. It was in the syllables of the phrase "Man up, big boys don't cry" that I prepared my home. Still to this day, regardless of the work I have done to detoxify my masculinity, I still find myself acutely aware of my exposed vulnerabilities. I'm sure, throughout the pages of this book, you noticed the frequency in which I used man up, big boys don't cry. Truth is, at every instance of the phrasing, marked tears ran down my face as I penned this work.

Yet, with every tear that ran down my face, growth accompanied the rejuvenating fluid to the soil in which the seeds of my purpose are planted. It is in the vulnerability of God-ordained manhood that my harvest abounds. In writing this book, while encased in the dull grey walls of a cold prison cell, I have found a level of freedom that can only be amassed once purpose has been actualized. Truth is: toxic masculinity did its very best to divert me from who it is I am called to be. Luckily, God loved me more than I loved masculinity.

Just as God loved me, He loves you, and the scars you bear from masculinity's doing can all be nullified by beginning the man-down process. For those who haven't been taking notes, let's run through the steps.

1. Identification: Seek to name the need in which you are looking to meet. It is in the identification of your needs that you can begin to create a working vocabulary. This vocabulary affords the opportunity to relay our needs to those we cherish most. If we operate outside of the knowledge of known needs, we are subject to fall victim to the guise of toxic masculinity.

2. Emotional intelligence: Understand that your emotions are not only necessary, but they are welcomed. We,

as men, are often told that emotions signify a sign of weakness. Yet, the truth lies in the fact that emotions are the only avenue to God-ordained manhood. It is only in love, in contrition, and in adoration that we can begin to walk tall in the manhood we were meant to achieve.

3. Purposeful behavior: Win on purpose! Begin to live your life in accordance with the need you have the desire to meet. Purposeful behavior most often resides at the intersection of purpose and opportunity. It is in the step of purposeful behavior that we have not only begun to detoxify but are now walking throughout our lives living according to God's ordained plan for manhood.

4. Forgiveness: Understand the faults of others do not define your worth. Although you may have been hurt, cheated on, lied to, and manipulated, none of it symbolizes the love that you deserve. So, understand that forgiveness is necessary because most often, in these times, you are learning something that you would most likely not have learned any other way.

5. Man down: Both physically and metaphorically. There will be times where you must find yourself on your knees, face down in prayer. It is in this prostrate position that you are most vulnerable. It is here that we begin to give up our perceived control and begin to seek

God's designs for the ordination of manhood. While often the most difficult phase of the man-down process, it becomes the most liberating. Only through true relationship with God can we become the man that He knows us to be. As a matter of fact, while we are at it, let's make this number one as well!

Listen, it is dire for the advancement of the God-ordained man that we not only seek detoxification for ourselves but those around us. Instead of telling our brothers to "man up, big boys don't cry," we should tell them to man down because John 11:15 tells us that even Jesus wept. There is something beautiful in the embracing of your emotions. What is more, there is something beautiful in living according to your purpose. We must begin the task to man down; while a daunting one, it is necessary to the success of humanity. It is through the lens of God's ordained manhood that we can begin to access all that God has for us.

Understand that I am just like you. I have been in some of the very same positions you have been in, and maybe even some worse ones. I have known hurt, abandonment, and fear. But which is more, through the transformative power of detoxifying my masculinity, I have amassed a level of freedom that can only be achieved in the embracing of emotions. As I told my amazing wife in the courtroom, if I can change one person's life with my story, then it was all worth it. Hopefully, your life has been changed as you begin the work to man down because even Jesus wept.